T0178714

Cybercrime and Cyberwarfare

FOCUS SERIES

Series Editor Jean-Charles Pomerol

Cybercrime and Cyberwarfare

Igor Bernik

WILEY

First published 2014 in Great Britain and the United States by ISTE Ltd and John Wiley & Sons, Inc.

ISTE Ltd
27-37 St George's Road
London SW19 4EU
UK

www.iste.co.uk

John Wiley & Sons, Inc.
111 River Street
Hoboken, NJ 07030
USA

www.wiley.com

Library of Congress Control Number: 2013952661

British Library Cataloguing-in-Publication Data
A CIP record for this book is available from the British Library
ISSN 2051-2481 (Print)
ISSN 2051-249X (Online)
ISBN 978-1-84821-671-6

Contents

Introduction

This book is based on monitoring, examining and researching areas that deal with information security, i.e. cybercrime and cyberwarfare. These represent a major contemporary challenge for professionals and the general public, since relative fear and misunderstanding are still present due to new developments in this area. The purpose of this book is to alert, raise awareness, eliminate myths and promote reflection on this particular social issue. The author's interest in this issue inspired the writing of this book, which aims to transfer and present a theoretical basis and understanding to the reader.

The development of information science and information and communication technology has resulted in users conducting their daily work in cyberspace and has led to their critical dependence on the technologies and contents that are accessible at all times. Since a lot of activities were transferred from the real world into cyberspace, crime has also adapted to these changes. In the beginning, individuals tried to prove that intrusion into information systems was possible, and with the development of systems and technologies, as well as with the aforementioned relocation of activities, cyberspace was also detected by criminal groups. They initially applied the possible options only to communicate with each other, but later they also started committing crimes in cyberspace. Further developments have shown that cyberspace is a great platform into which one can transfer activities from the real world (e.g. business) and where the committing of certain types of crime is even easier. It provides greater anonymity, and offenses are more difficult to detect and prosecute. The main reasons for this are the global orientation of cyberspace, the ambiguity of legal norms and the possibility of transferring illegal activities to parts of the world where they are permitted or where the perpetrators are simply not prosecuted.

Information security and cyberwarfare are important not only at the organizational level but also at the state level because the national information infrastructure is an increasing risk factor which is constantly under threat. Achieving foreign policy goals, creating and developing international relations and international economic cooperation has never been more easily achieved than today when the world is critically dependent on information technology (IT). National critical infrastructure provides a sense of security, autonomy and sovereignty for companies, which are the main contributing factors for the stability of a certain country. By misusing and destructing these attributes, the achievement of foreign policy goals becomes extremely simple. This key vulnerability of modern society is often the target of state and military cyberwarriors. Not only organizations but also states must provide an understanding of the nature of cybercrime and related cyberwarfare if they want to ensure an adequate level of security for the population.

Since criminal acts in cyberspace rely on the same type of legal acts in the event of prosecution (the same laws, rules, etc.) and since cyberwarfare is generally considered as an example of organized crime, cybercrime and cyberwarfare are presented in this book with an emphasis on the need for their mutual differentiation, both at the international

political level and at the legislative level. The latter
represents the basis for further proceedings and problem-
solving. It is necessary to harmonize legislative acts and
adapt them to the severity and risk of various forms of
cybercrime. Without this, any action is doomed to failure.
Because of the current legislative situation, cybercrime is
easier to commit than to prosecute.

As may be observed from the topics covered, the author
sees cybercrime and cyberwarfare as areas that are
developing exponentially and threatening everyday work and
business, and thus an understanding of these topics is
necessary to ensure the appropriate level of information
security. On the basis of experience, the author observes that
this book will provide added value to a wide range of
potential users: management executives who with their
knowledge of modern guidelines influence (offensive or
defensive) security strategies, experts in (information)
security and modern crime, chief information officers,
specialized law enforcement authorities and readers who are
interested in such developments in cyberspace.

Acknowledgement

This book would not have been possible without the strong support of the Faculty of Criminal Justice and Security, University of Maribor, and participating individuals.

Cybercrime

In the two decades following the widespread use of the Internet, it has grown from a network that linked a few enthusiasts to become the essential element of modern life for millions of people [UNO 10]. In the late modern age, the world has become completely dependent on Internet access and sharing information over the Internet, while in recent years other forms of communication that join and connect people in global cyberspace[1] have been added. New connectivity options and changed ways of working have brought about new forms of threats, which impact the privacy and security of users when using cyberspace.

The dangers of cyberspace were first mentioned when new technologies emerged, which allowed not only communication, but also the performance of daily tasks. This enabled the growth of the Internet and various services such as shopping, paying for goods and services, online banking, sending files, data transfer and other forms of work with the help of the Internet, connections with mobile devices and

1 A metaphor for describing the non-physical terrain created by computer systems. Online systems, for example, create a cyberspace within which people can communicate with one another (via e-mail), do research or simply window shop. Like physical space, cyberspace contains objects (files, mail messages, graphics, etc.) and different modes of transportation and delivery. Unlike real space, though, exploring cyberspace does not require any physical movement other than pressing keys on a keyboard or moving a mouse. The term was coined by author William Gibson in his science-fiction novel *Neuromancer* in 1984 [CYB 13].

constant access to and interaction with global cyberspace. Eventually, all this became self-evident and was perceived as an everyday occurrence. Personal and business data, such as various security passwords, with which criminals can obtain proprietary information and inflict a lot of damage, have become a magnet for invaders. If one becomes a victim of cyberthieves, the consequences are far from amusing, since one can directly or indirectly lose a lot of money. Seizures that are not even perceived by users, as they do not even know that someone is "walking" in their information system, are even more dangerous [NEU 06]. This is why information security systems started to be created, as the use of computers and mobile devices – and their connection to the Internet and to the rest of cyberspace, as well as the permanent exchange of information – has become a fixture of our everyday lives.

With the advent of cyberspace, access to information and connections among users has completely changed, which significantly affects the work, communication practices and behavior of society. The changing working methods, the use of cyberspace to perform various activities and the transfer of data into cyberspace also contribute to the migration of different types of crimes to cyberspace[2]. While known types of crime are migrating into this new environment, new types of crime related to cyberspace are also appearing. The most recent forms of crime to energe are associated with online social networks, as "the amount of personal information that individuals share and publish on the Internet is growing rapidly, especially due to the increasing popularity of online social networks" [DIM 10, p. 395], and with financial fraud committed both in cyberspace and in real space [IOC 11, DIO 11].

---

2 The first online attacks, occurred in the United States in the 1970s, during the development of the inter-network system, the forerunner of today's Internet.

In modern work habits, where a permanent link to cyberspace is necessary, most abuse is "allowed" due to the ignorance or indifference of people who use computers connected to the Internet, for they mostly deal with information resources unconscientiously [MCC 05]. A greater deal of knowledge and experience, a higher level of awareness and a better protection of computers with elementary programs and security tools contribute to lowering the risk. People who spend more time working seriously with a computer and are aware of the safety and value of stored data also devote more time to protect such data, and consequently feel less threatened even though they are more exposed. "The security of the increasingly important information systems in our societies covers many aspects, of which the fight against cybercrime is a core element. Without an agreed definition of cybercrime, the terms 'cybercrime', 'computer crime', 'computer-related crime' or 'high-tech crime' are often used interchangeably" [ECO 07].

According to certain estimates (e.g. [SEC 10]), the financial benefit of cybercrime is enormous. However, some experts do not agree with such claims, since Anderson *et al.* [AND 12] believe that the benefit is decent, but rarely comparable to the high incomes of traditional crime. However, if we consider that in mid-2012, there were already 2.4 billion Internet users, or 34.3% of the world population [INT 12], and if only a small percentage of them were naive and abused, cybercrime[3] has enough room for further development.

Because of the expected financial benefits, the amount of funds for the committing of cybercrime is growing steadily, since profits are also increasing. In light of the economic problems faced by the developing world, the issue is ever growing. Criminals obtain money and valuable data from people who believe in making a quick and easy profit using

---

3 Cybercrime: the use of information and communication technologies to carry out criminal, harmful and immoral acts in cyberspace.

various tricks, since there are always plenty of naive victims. Despite a greater awareness among users, there are more and more victims. The techniques used for the committing of crime in cyberspace are becoming increasingly sophisticated as cybercriminals collaborate with a growing number of educated people who cannot get appropriate employment or adequate payment for their work. This has created several large organized groups that dominate cyberspace and as Professor Ross Anderson, who participated in the preparation of a general model for calculating the costs of cybercrime, states: "A small number of gangs lie behind many incidents and locking them up would be far more effective than telling the public to fit an antiphishing toolbar or purchase antivirus software" [AND 12].

Because a large number of users have very limited knowledge of how the technology works and the potential dangers of cyberspace, and are, at the same time, naive enough and wish to earn or progress quickly, the testing ground for cybercriminals is practically endless. Most cyberspace users are thus threatened by attacks and subsequent abuse. To reduce and raise awareness of safety risks, we have a possibility to use a variety of methods and techniques for ensuring information security, which aim to reduce the threat and the number of realized attacks through preventive efforts. In terms of information security, we are constantly searching for a balance between security and functionality. A large degree of safety and security causes a number of problems within the organization itself, because employees are unable to access the desired resources they need for conducting their business quickly and easily, while on the other hand, a large degree of flexibility facilitates unauthorized access to confidential sources of the company by potential internal attackers.

Large and economically powerful countries, such as the United States, China and Australia, or certain major European countries (Germany, France and the United

Kingdom) can afford specific services and/or police departments to prosecute cybercrime. Smaller and economically weaker countries, such as Slovenia or Bosnia and Herzegovina and others, which alongside limited economic capacities also have a limited (small) number of experts in the field of information technology (IT) and information security and cannot afford a specific police department, consequently have to cooperate and establish links with other countries [FBI 11]. On January 1, 2013, EUROPOL founded the EC3 – European Cybercrime Centre [EC3 13], in order to assist countries in combating cybercrime and to improve mutual cooperation between countries within the EU. This center is responsible for the protection of European citizens using cyberspace. Due to the nature of cyberattacks, in which an attacker from Russia, China, Australia, Brazil or in fact from anywhere in the world can attack a company in the United States, Slovenia, Bosnia and Herzegovina or Germany by using their regular computer connected to the Internet, international cooperation between investigative and law-enforcement authorities (FBI, EUROPOL, NATO and state institutions) and information sharing is thus even more important.

Cyberattacks are extremely fast and can affect thousands or even millions of electronic devices[4] within moments anywhere in the world. Individuals and companies need to be careful because all of their knowledge, information about consumers and customers, plans and products that are kept as trade secrets can pass into the hands of competitors, domestic or foreign intelligence services, and other villains in a split second.

---

4 Recently, experts in the field of cybercrime only spoke of threats to computers and the data stored on them. With the growth of mobile telephony and the use of many other electronic devices to connect to the Internet, it is necessary to expand this concept to all electronic devices that can be connected to the Internet or that are capable of mutual electronic communication, including, e.g., devices for electronic control of dialysis or electronic cardiac control systems, where a cyberattack could jeopardize the health of patients.

In addition to external attacks on information and organizations' information systems, employees of the organization also have a lot of opportunities for accessing classified information, which expands the possibilities of abuse both by people who are authorized and have access to confidential information, as well as employees who do not have such powers. Internal attacks in organizations are more difficult to detect than attacks from outside, and it is even harder to respond to them. A wrong response can impair mutual relations and arouse distrust among employees. A theft or transmission of confidential information from a company can, in case there is an internal attacker, be understood as a deliberate abuse of information and communication systems, authorized and unauthorized users or as a human error. Employees are not only dangerous because of their malicious thoughts and actions directed against the company, but also because of their ignorance and negligence, which is why IT specialists often claim that the most secure computer is the computer that is not included in the network and not used by anyone. This, of course, makes no sense because such a system is useless in the modern world and cannot meet the needs of work-related activities. By using various methods of social engineering[5], a potential attacker convinces an individual within the company to do something that allows him/her to access the data [MIT 11]. To avoid the security measures of the company, an attacker has to convince the user to entrust him/her with the data, which he/she can use to log into the attacked system. Successful attackers usually have good communication skills, are charming, friendly and able to quickly establish a trusting relationship. For this reason, people remain the weakest link in the security chain and are often ignored when preparing security policies and procedures. To avoid threats by attackers using social engineering, we need to invest in preventive measures, such

---

5 Social engineering often denotes the art of manipulation or persuasion of people to do something or disclose confidential information [GOO 10].

as in-house education, and improve training for users. Employees, contract workers and all others who have access to organizational systems and services must be fully informed of the importance of security and the steps they need to take in order to keep the information and communication system safe. All employees and other users associated with the information system of a certain organization need to be aware of the general information security policy and understand their role in providing security for the organization.

The process of updating services also changes the information security policy, and hence information security[6] as such. In doing so, organizations must be careful to keep employees informed about changes and potential threats. Information and security policy should clearly define what happens if someone in the company intentionally or accidentally breaches the rules on information and security. The consequences must be clear and convincing in order to point out the gravity and their potential for realization. The security strategy determined by people responsible for security within the company is usually sacrificed on account of questions about how to persuade the executives and users of the company to implement it. If the heads of the information security departments had adequate resources to ensure an appropriate level of information security, they could prevent the realization of threats. It often happens that organizations, which have never been a victim of an information incident[7], encounter great difficulties when justifying investments or obtaining management support for projects that would ensure an appropriate security level. The real information security problem solving is provided only by a comprehensive security strategy of the organization rather

---

6 Information security: protecting data from unauthorized access or modification, in order to guarantee their availability, confidentiality and integrity.
7 An information incident is any unauthorized access to sensitive information [UWM 11].

than by solving their individual parts. Cybercrime perpetrators are becoming more experienced every day and use a number of techniques that are relatively unknown, which forces defense to always be one step behind the attackers. In particular, the integrity, care and handling of information security as an unfinished process can be the only defense against information and security incidents.

With the penetration of information and communication technologies (ICTs) to almost all areas of human activity and with the increasing number of IT users, IT is becoming ever more common and the most popular target for criminals. Attacks are becoming more numerous, more sophisticated and they inflict more damage.

The regulation of cyberspace within criminal law lags behind technological development [ZAV 08], and there are also problems related to cooperation between the countries in the fight against cybercrime, which is highly international. Therefore, the initiatives undertaken by EUROPOL, the FBI, NATO and similar organizations contribute to the prevention, prosecution and reduction of threats posed by cybercrime, and provide greater safety for users.

Crimes in cyberspace are characterized by the fact that the damage caused is unclear and it is difficult to determine its financial consequences. Contemporary approaches to measuring the cost of cybercrime [AND 12] demonstrate methods for the realistic assessment of damage. However, in the overall treatment of cybercrime, there are still problems related to the corroboration of attacks, the cause of damage and the identification of perpetrators, which is why many such acts remain unreported, unpursued and the perpetrators remain at large [WAL 08].

Despite the general view that cybercrime emerged in recent years with the increasing use of the Internet, it has to be pointed out that it was already present in the past. It developed together with cyberspace and ICT. Its scope extended in parallel with the development of technology. In the past, the main motive of perpetrators was to prove that no system is completely secure, because each of them has critical points that perpetrators are able to detect and abuse the possibility of intrusion. Initially, the main motive of cybercrime perpetrators was amusement, curiosity, etc., while today they operate primarily for profit or money they obtain from data and identity thefts, the majority of attacks directly enable the gain of financial resources, especially from online fraud. It could, therefore, be said that most crimes committed in cyberspace today are financially conditioned. Perpetrators committing fraud are collecting financial assets of uninformed or careless users by acquiring confidential information and then blackmailing them, or by stealing money from their bank accounts. An increase in white-collar cybercrime, i.e. offenses related to various types of sophisticated cyberfrauds, carried out by organized groups of cyberattackers [IOC 11] is also observed. Although the white-collar crime is usually associated with the executive management of organizations, cyberspace in this segment joins people from various fields who use different cheating techniques in cyberspace [O'CO 11]. In doing so, they, for example, misuse intercepted information or information on credit cards obtained by hacking, use different methods of phishing, installing malware, etc., in order to obtain unlawful proceeds or to launder the money of innocent victims by misusing the information obtained.

Many ways of attacking ICT are thus developed, and all attacks have negative consequences and cause damage to targets or victims. There are many programs developed to combat this type of attack, but cybercrime perpetrators are already so skillful that no user protection program can stop them. In the future, the number of attacks will only increase, and new technologies and methods for committing cybercrime will be developed [UNO 10]. One has to be aware of the fact that information systems[8], networks and communication devices are becoming increasingly connected. These kinds of connections consequently increase the number of opportunities for entry into, manipulation, obstruction, destruction and theft of the data stored in a system or transmitted between interconnected systems. Today's society is highly dependent on networks, data flows and the electronic automation of several work-related operations, which is why it is extremely vulnerable. Global vulnerability of the "networked" society can be observed in cases of data theft, online fraud, the spreading of malware and inoperative systems, as well as in the amount of estimated loss, which is measured in millions [IC3 10a, PON 12]. Electronic devices which interconnect and transfer data to or through the Internet are just an additional tool for the perpetrators, an accessory to commit criminal offenses in cyberspace. The Internet gives them a global dimension, enables them to stay anonymous and communicate directly and safely, opens the way to knowledge, generates a large number of victims and gives a plethora of opportunities and assistance for carrying out illegal transactions.

The prosecution of criminal offenses in cyberspace is problematic as it is always necessary to adapt the methods of detection, investigation and guaranteeing proof. Apart from that, people even decide not to report many cybercrime offenses. Often they do so because they completely overlook the offenses or believe that they are to blame for the abuse. Organizations that have been abused often believe that in order to protect their reputation and confidence in their operations it is futile to report cyberattacks, their potential damage or consequences. Thus, they additionally contribute to the growth of cybercrime, since the perpetrators do not feel themselves to be at risk.

---

8 Information system: integrity of components for the collection, processing, dissemination and storage of information.

The phrase *cybercrime* denotes various types of crimes, among which the majority are indeed criminal; however, this phrase also encompasses certain acts committed in cyberspace, which in some cases are not (yet) punishable under the national penal law or international legal acts. Or as Wall [WAL 09] states, in defining the extent of cybercrime, an explanation of what exactly constitutes a "cybercrime" is missing, since the offenses are set out in criminal codes regardless of the "space" in which they are carried out, the way in which they are committed and how they occur. Users of cyberspace often expect adjusted regulations in response to cybercrime, but this is unreasonable, as many actions are already defined in the criminal laws of individual countries. These also allow the prosecution of offenses committed in cyberspace, such as child pornography, stealing money from bank accounts, fraud and abuse.

However, for a comprehensive understanding of cybercrime it is necessary to understand a complex contrast: among hundreds of thousands of attacks which are reported every year by the cyber or information-security branches, the number of prosecutions is still relatively low [WAL 08, AND 12]. Due to the special nature of cybercrime, only a very small number of crimes committed in cyberspace are prosecuted, although, as Zavrsnik [ZAV 08] states, "the assumption of anonymity on the Internet is history, since all activities performed on it are recorded". Perpetrators of cybercrime are well versed in and are properly able to hide their identity, so that investigators are unable to discover who carries out the offenses. Finding the perpetrators in cyberspace may seem very easy to laymen and those unaware of network technologies. In reality, however, the complexity of technology and the global nature of cyberspace make their detection extremely difficult. The power of formal social control is significantly weaker in complex criminal cases than, for example, in cases of conventional property and violent crime. Responding to cybercrime requires specialization and special training for gathering evidence, as well as adequate control and punishment of cybercriminals. The problem lies in the ambiguous definition of cybercrime and in determining which actions should actually be punished. To provide the general safety and carefree use of technologies and cyberspace, it is necessary to address the following important issues: is the fear of cybercrime justified?; how much threat does it actually pose to people?; and what could be done to reduce the risk or the victimization of users?

The term "cybercrime" describes various offenses. These include offenses related to the misuse of data and computer systems (hacking); the forgeries and frauds committed by the use of a computer (phishing); offenses regarding the redistribution of unauthorized content (dissemination of child pornography) and copyright infringements (distribution of pirated content) [UNO 10]. According to EUROPOL [EUR 07], which summarizes the Convention on Cybercrime [COC 01], the definition of cybercrime includes "crimes against the Confidentiality, Integrity and Availability of computer data and systems, computer related traditional crimes, content-related offences, offences related to infringement of copyright and related rights, infringement of privacy".

Cybercrime is considered to be a crime consisting of offenses for which the IT (personal and tablet PC, smart phones, game consoles and other electronic devices that allow the connection to and exchange of data with cyberspace) represents both a tool or an object of the attack, and for the committing or attempt to commit such a crime, a certain knowledge of computer or information science is required.

Therefore, cybercrime is perceived as a criminal use of a computer network or of other systems on the Internet, an attack or misuse of systems and networks to carry out criminal offenses, and abuse committed by the use of new technologies, or new criminal offenses, which constantly develop in cyberspace. In the author's opinion, cybercrime is the most appropriate term to describe criminal offenses related to computers and networks. This concept takes into account the fact that a criminal offense is connected with computers and committed in cyberspace [ZAV 05]. Furthermore, "cybercrime also involves harmful and immoral acts in cyberspace that are not always criminalized and punishable" [PER 09]. Communities in cyberspace, victimization and victims of cyberspace, particularities of cybercrime perpetrators and violence in cyberspace are all elements that depend on the perception of cybercrime, awareness of this phenomenon and fear of it. The term "cybercrime" therefore relates to acts that are committed by means of electronic data processing equipment and induce undesirable effects. This encompasses any unlawful activity, which includes copying, removal, interference, intrusion, destruction or other manipulation with a computer system, computer, data or computer programs [ZAV 07]. Therefore, the phenomenon of cybercrime has to be analyzed from the perspective of perpetrators, victims and circumstances of the criminal offense. In addition, the fear of the crime, which greatly affects the perception of negative events and people's response to them, has to be considered as well. The fear of certain types of crime does not exist if people do not know of certain sources of threats, while on the other hand, increasing people's sensitivity to a particular type of deviant behavior is a cause for their excessive response to information security threats [ZAV 10]. When considering the definition of [ALS 05], which states that cybercrime is hidden, that it uses the network (in a non-physical sense) and occasionally leads to profit, and taking into account the elements of cybercrime as defined in the international Convention on Cybercrime concerning the criminalization of racist and xenophobic acts committed through computer systems [COC 01], the author proposes a simple and modern definition of cybercrime:

Cybercrime is the use of ICTs to carry out criminal, harmful and immoral acts in cyberspace.

Criminal offenses in cyberspace are often not an isolated event, but can also be a part of a larger criminal offense at the physical level. The proliferation of the Internet and its general social acceptance have greatly increased the number of victims (including by type), which can now be found all over the world, ranging from military, governmental and educational institutions, enterprises and other business users, and companies that provide care for infrastructure and Internet services to individual Internet users, and critical types of social infrastructure (electricity, water, fuel and emergency medical services). One of the major challenges faced by law enforcement agencies in combating international cybercrime is their ability to effectively co-ordinate investigations between various authorities and legal systems.

Events in cyberspace occur faster than events in the "normal" world. Taking business decisions, finding information and personal contacts on the Internet are thus faster than usual. The perpetrators are aware of this and exploit the possibilities of the Internet. They can send e-mails around the world or post information on Websites that are instantly available everywhere in a matter of seconds, and thus commit fraud a lot faster than they used to. Most e-mail users have already received an e-mail in which they were offered various financial benefits or were provided with an unusual business proposal. In these e-mails, perpetrators usually promise a quick and easy profit, sell goods at incredibly low prices or even offer services free of charge. The most common examples of cybercrime include (summarized and complemented according to [YAR 06], [FBI 11] and [AND 12]):

– Political intrusions and cyberwarfare:

   - industrial cyberespionage and extortion;

   - cyberterrorism;

   - information warfare.

– Virtual piracy:

   - copyright-infringing software;

   - copyright-infringing music and video.

– Cyberfraud:

   - identity theft;

   - online payment card fraud;

   - online banking fraud;

   - in-person payment card fraud;

   - fake antivirus;

   - infringing pharmaceuticals;

   - "stranded traveler" scams,

   - "fake escrow" scams;

   - advanced fee fraud;

   - Nigerian Letter or "419" Fraud;

   - Private Automatic Branch Exchange (PABX)[9] fraud;

   - fiscal fraud;

   - other commercial fraud.

– Illegal, harmful and offensive Website content:

   - child pornography;

   - hate speech.

---

9 PABX or Toll Fraud is the illegal and unauthorized use of telephone equipment, telephone lines and services in order to make expensive and numerous long-distance calls that are charged to attacked organization or person.

– Victimization of individuals on the Internet:

- distributing of indecent material;

- Internet grooming;

- stalking;

- harassment;

- extortion;

- pedophilia.

To prepare a model of cybercrime costs in the United Kingdom, the causal model of the different types of cybercrime (Figure 1.1.) summarizes and interconnects the aforementioned points, and thus fully addresses the causal and consequential links related to cybercrime, as well as the aspects regarding citizens, businesses and governments.

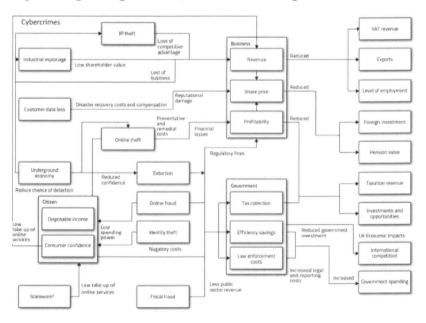

Figure 1.1. *Causal model of the different types of cybercrime [DET 11]*

Irrespective of their importance, the authors have deliberately left out the following types of cybercrime from this model:

– cyberbullying;

– distributing indecent material;

– selling counterfeit goods;

– the financial effects of peer-to-peer file-sharing;

– using the profits of cybercrime to fund more conventional crime;

– other non-financially oriented criminal activity conducted online, such as Internet grooming.

These types of cybercrime were not relevant to the presented study, under which the model was created. They did, however, clearly distinguish between financially motivated cybercrime, cyberwarfare and cyberterrorism[10].

In addition to these areas, the scope of cybercrime can also include critical information networks or important social infrastructure that is of vital importance nowadays and upon which the modern society is largely dependent. These include the fields of telecommunications, banking and finance, transportation and distribution, water, electricity and gas supply, military and police facilities, emergency services and information services [EUR 07]. As already noted, society has become extremely vulnerable due to its high dependence on technology, and an attack on information systems that maintain and ensure the proper functioning of technologies can also threaten lives, cause a lot of financial damage or paralyze the functioning of society.

---

10 Cyberterrorism: premeditated, politically motivated attack using ICT in cyberspace to attack other information and communication systems (computers, information systems, computer programs, databases or data) with the aim of causing panic, fear, large-scale public responses and possibly deaths.

All of the above is especially true for potential attacks on critical infrastructure, which is why its protection has a special place in ensuring cybersecurity.

The methods of carrying out attacks will not be described in detail in this section, but individual methods will be mentioned and briefly described through examples (phishing, social engineering, etc.). It should be emphasized that various works in the field of information/cybersecurity present most of the known methods employed for carrying out attacks, while new methods are emerging almost daily and are regularly published by various sources, available primarily on the Internet, e.g. Info World, Security Week, IEEE Spectrum[11] and similar. Those who are interested in these topics can learn in detail about the execution of each attack with the help of these sources. Since this kind of detail does not provide a better understanding of cybercrime, no such descriptions are included in this section.

The increasing use of modern technologies, which mainly occurred due to the affordability of equipment and consequently produced a large number of cyberspace users, contributed to the use of computers and other electronic devices in a wide range of criminal offenses. The role of ICT and electronic devices in criminal offenses is divided into the following sections (modified and complemented according to [EUR 07] and [ROC 08]):

– ICT as a tool to commit a criminal offense:

  - intrusion into a computer or other electronic system;

  - deleting, modifying and/or entering data into the device under attack;

  - disabling or obstructing networks;

  - information, password and credit card number theft;

---

11 www.infoworld.com, www.securityweek.com and spectrum.ieee.org.

- exchange of child pornography;

- participation in online chat rooms and the arrangement of meetings with children;

- online banking fraud;

- forgery of checks and credit cards;

- fraudulent or deceptive advertising and sales;

- pyramid schemes;

- intellectual property theft.

– ICT as a target of a criminal offense:

In this case, technology is a target of criminal offenses. Electronic devices are mostly interesting because of the data they hold. This study will present the cases of industrial espionage[12] and cyberwarfare, which are both rapidly increasing especially in the industrially and informationally developed countries. An electronic device thus becomes a target when:

- it keeps confidential information;

- it contains trade secrets;

- the offender wishes to obtain free services that are enabled by the device;

- an electronic device is used as an intermediary to attack other electronic devices.

– ICT as devices that store evidence of a criminal offense:

Due to the prevalence of modern electronic devices in the economy, in households and with the perpetrators of criminal offences, such devices contain important information that can be used as evidence in pretrial or

---

12 Industrial espionage: obtaining information on plans, products, processes and customers of competitive organizations, most often in an illegal way.

criminal proceedings in an increasing number of cases. Various lists, directories, business records and other documentation mostly switched from paper to electronic formats. These data often include:

- lists of personal data;

- employee work calendars and project development data;

- databases;

- e-mails;

- letters, contracts and agreements;

- photographs (e.g. child pornography and discrediting);

- financial data.

– ICT as an assistance to law enforcement authorities:

Electronic devices can be a great tool for law enforcement authorities in detecting, investigating and providing proof of criminal offences. The following tools are very helpful:

- databases of transactions and operations;

- tables of financial transactions;

- search tools on the Internet;

- various simulations;

- various analytical software.

ICT can therefore be used both for the committing and investigation of criminal offences. Modern technology can thus be used in a wide variety of ways, since the committing of cybercrime is discovered primarily with the same or similar methods that were used for its perpetration. In August 2007, a EUROPOL report entitled "High-Tech Crimes within the EU" drew attention to the vertical and horizontal uses of high technology "in order to give some insights and to facilitate the comprehension of the threat". This report "aims to deal with the issue facing two parallel, but at many times convergent, subjects: the communities of cybercriminals and the use of hi-tech by criminal organizations. In other words, one part is dedicated to the organized groups who attack computer systems for various reasons in order to understand what kind of threats can be expected. The second part is focused on the use criminal organizations can make of high technology: utilizing new tools and techniques or even using the skills of cybercriminals, recruiting or simply hiring them; in other words: the horizontal use of hi-tech." [EUR 07]:

– "The vertical use of hi-tech occurs when the computer (or computer network) is the target of the criminal activity as the final goal. Spamming[13], hacking[14] and crimewares[15] are just some examples in which the presence of the machine is fundamental for the existence of the crime.

– The horizontal use of hi-tech is when the computer is utilized as a tool in order to facilitate criminals' goals".

When considering these acts of cybercrime, it becomes clear that technology took over the position of other "tools" that had been used to commit criminal offenses in the past. However, since the investigation of criminal offenses usually uses similar countermeasures as the perpetration of criminal acts, we cannot ignore the role of network infrastructure, computers, electronic devices and, in particular, data sources, which are very different due to recent developments (hard drives, USB sticks, memory cards, flash memory, tapes and cloud storage). At the same time, access to some of the

---

13 Spamming: sending unwanted e-mails to reduce the availability of the mailbox and motivate users for data transmission.
14 Hacking: intrusion into information systems at all levels. (Unauthorized) use or access to computer systems or network resources in order to get knowledge of or access to the information system. Ethical hacking denotes a deliberately unauthorized use of systems to identify system deficiencies.
15 Crimewares: special computer code or programs to implement cybercrime.

data sources is very difficult, especially to cloud data storage, which makes the detection and prosecution of offenders difficult and requires a lot of knowledge.

1.1. The perpetrators of cybercrime

The number of perpetrators of cybercrime as well as the damage they cause is constantly growing. In 2000, Gartner predicted a 1,000% increase in damage over the next 4 years [DEM 03]. For these reasons, Dobovsek [DOB 09] notes that cybercrime can "easily be ranked among the most dangerous and socially harmful forms of modern crime". A much appreciated characteristic of the Internet, i.e. the ability to hide or misrepresent one's identity, is the main reason for such a situation. The Internet enables everyone to be whoever they want to be online, which means that it is relatively difficult to detect the true identity of the person who has, for example, stolen credit card numbers from the bank or attacked a Website and thus prevented its functioning.

The question of identity is justified by the reasonableness of introducing certain restrictions on the use of the Internet. The Internet provides a certain anonymity for users, which is not bad as such (since it enables uncensored reporting, unlimited political communication, public and private discussions on problematic social issues, or unpleasant personal problems, etc.). Anonymity and pseudonymity in this respect demonstrate the rights of individuals to privacy, while at the same time highlight the conflict of interests between the individual and society, since abuse is the price that the society has to pay in order to preserve benefits. In particular, the possibility to hide one's identity can be attributed to some of the worst cases of abuse in cyberspace, which was already found by Kabay [KAB 98]. The situation related to the spread of cybercrime in recent years became even worse due to more sophisticated methods of attack and refined forms of misuse, large numbers of users and cases of identity misuse.

The methods of attacks vary considerably in terms of risk, costs and complexity. The perpetrators often prefer to choose low-risk attacks and thus gain lower revenues from their criminal offenses. The amount of revenues is one of the measures on the basis of which offenders can be classified, but it has to be noted that there are also large differences in the way they are organized. It could be stated that the better the perpetrators are organized, interconnected and the more assets they invest, the higher their profits. This is well illustrated by the following scale, which ranks various types of offenders into four groups from the highest to the lowest level [DET 11]:

– Foreign intelligence services may have a substantial impact on the economy by sponsoring or engaging directly in widespread industrial espionage. This type of cybercriminal tends to be highly organized, with sophisticated techniques and extensive resources.

– Large organized crime networks are focusing more of their attention on cybercrime because it offers attractive rewards for minimal investment and low risk.

– Disreputable but legitimate organizations may engage in cybercrimes such as IP theft or industrial espionage to obtain a rival company's sensitive information.

– Individuals or small groups of opportunistic cybercriminals will tend to target citizens and vulnerable organizations.

The development of computer technology and the emergence of communication between computers showed, in the 1980s, that when individuals who communicate with each other do not know each other (are anonymous), the phenomenon of deindividuation may appear, resulting in increasingly antisocial behavior. When deindividuated, an individual cannot control his/her own behavior anymore due to perceived anonymity. Various studies suggest that due to their anonymity, it is more likely that people will behave aggressively (e.g. [PER 09]). The latest version of the deindividuation theory – social identity theory of deindividuation (SIDE) – argues that the personality is divided into two parts: personal identity, with individual characteristics, and social identity, which comes to the fore in a particular group. Individuals will behave in a deviant way, if their social or group identity supports and encourages this kind of behavior and vice versa [WIL 08]. Perhaps users feel "hidden" among so many other people or believe they are immersed in the vast cyberspace, made up of millions of users connected to the Internet. They see themselves more as a part of this large group than as individuals. They are aware of the relative distance from others and relative immunity from identification and sanctions. An individual in cyberspace is also "deaf" or is not aware of the significance of their acts and their consequences in the real world. An eventual pirate on the Internet does not feel the need to "consider their contested decisions" and does not feel obligated to "control the tendency to commit an unconventional offense" [HIN 08]. Anonymity and deindividuation play a certain role in the decision of an individual to carry out criminal offenses. It is thus impossible to assess whether the process of deindividuation itself "forced" the individual to show deviant behavior or whether they made this choice on the basis of a cost-benefit analysis (how much economic or other benefits the offense brings). The anonymity and deindividuation of cyberspace users alone are not the causes of deviant behavior, but can encourage individuals, who are already inclined to do so for one reason or another, to engage in such acts. Williams [WIL 08] believes that there would be a lot more crime if anonymity in itself caused deviant behavior. Although it seems that anonymity causes cybercrime; in reality, however, it is nothing else but a rational choice for those who are already predisposed to crime or deviant behavior. Regardless of the type of crime, its basis is certainly to maintain anonymity. Irrespective of the fact that someone acts as a pirate or a hacker, the offenses of both arise from the assumption that the discovery of their identity by the authorities is not very likely. If we also consider the commitment of authorities to prosecute this type of crime, we could observe that the fear of possible sanctions is almost non-existent. The combination of anonymity and low probability of sanctions is certainly the reason for individual forms of crime, which directly impair a certain person or more persons, an organization or even a country. Therefore, it seems that the role of anonymity and deindividuation in cybercrime cannot be viewed separately, which is somehow logical due to so many different forms of cybercrime. Some experts understand anonymity and deindividuation as the cause, while others believe it acts as a kind of catalyst. Given the fact that cybercrime is rapidly increasing, the aforementioned factors certainly play an important role, although this type of crime has not yet been precisely defined and studied.

1.1.1. *Motives of the perpetrators of cybercrime*

The motivation of an offender to commit a criminal offense differs from person to person; they may want to obtain reputation, self-confirmation, revenge and most often financial gain. We must not forget that cyberspace is an effective weapon in the hands of terrorists, politically motivated individuals and groups, and increasingly organized crime groups. Among others, active users and dealers of child pornography are also on the Internet. The IC3 report for 2010 [IC3 10b] shows that most cybercrimes originate from the United States (65.9%), followed by the United Kingdom (10.4%), Nigeria (5.8%), China (3.1%) and Canada (2.4%).

According to recent studies, the most common motivation of cybercrime perpetrators is to obtain material benefits [PON 11, PON 12, TRU 13], which result in large financial losses, especially for companies. Also, the data of identified offenders and other recent studies (e.g. [GAR 11]) suggest that the motives of perpetrators range from (self-) confirmation to obtaining material benefits. The main motive of perpetrators is thus a desire to make money, and this is also the main cause of modern cybercrime, especially identity theft, the use of spam and the installation or running of botnets[16].

In the event of cyberwarfare or cyberterrorism, motives are not directly linked with the acquisition of material benefits, but are broader and described further on in this work.

1.1.2. *Types of offenders*

Just as regular criminal offenses are committed by individuals or groups, cyberspace is also populated with individuals or groups that we are oblivious to because they use ICT. Nevertheless, we must not forget that a human being is responsible for every action in cyberspace. When it comes to "classic" criminal offenses, people have an idea of the actual perpetrator, but when it comes to cyberperpetrators, we somehow lose this actual image or do not even create one. It would thus be useful to start profiling cybercriminals and get to know their organization, just as this is done with the perpetrators of classic criminal offenses. This would help to dispel the myths and preconceptions that society and legislators have regarding cybercriminals. Not all of them are antisocial and live with their parents in the basement [HIG 08]. Many perpetrators of cybercrime are professional people who use their knowledge to achieve various goals. A study [BER 11b] showed that the classic stereotype of a young hacker who spends all their time in front of a computer and is not interested in their social environment is no longer true.

---

16 A botnet is a collection of compromised computers connected to the Internet, through which attacks are carried out.

A generic term used by the public for people who commit cybercrime is "hacker", but the subculture of perpetrators is much more divided and complex. There are several subgroups of offenders, which are divided according to different criteria, e.g. by their level of technical knowledge, field of interest and the use of software and hardware. These subgroups are further divided into narrower categories. A division of six basic categories is proposed [CHI 09]:

– *Toolkit newbies* are novices who only have little technical skills, use ready-made software and follow the documentation to guide them through the procedures of the programs.

– *Cyberpunks* can already create small programs that are used for defacing, spamming or stealing credit cards.

– *Internals* are employees or former employees who seek revenge; their main goal is to damage the system of the company and use the knowledge they have with regard to the security situation within the organization rather than technical knowledge.

– *Coders* are the creators of codes designed to damage other systems.

– *Old-guard hackers*, or hackers in short, have a high level of expertise and mostly do not have criminal intentions. They are more interested in the intellectual and cognitive side of hacking.

– *Professionals* are the most dangerous perpetrators of cybercrime. Their goal is always criminal in nature.

Even in the hacker underground, there are good and bad "players". In this respect, it is possible to distinguish between the following types of offenders [CHI 09]:

– *Black-hats* (as the very name suggests that they) are baddies who commit illegal acts, and their main purpose is to harm information systems, steal information, etc.

– *Gray-hats* are the so-called ethical hackers who do not want to belong to either bad or good players. In the past, some of them might have even dealt with the intrusion into information systems, but have decided to stop such practice.

– *White-hats* have the knowledge and skills that would enable them to function in the same way as black-hats, but they decided to be on the right side of the law. To this end, they often cooperate with the authorities and companies and work with them in order to combat cybercrime. In the past, they rarely engaged in illegal attacks on information systems.

According to the classification described above, there are only three main groups, but, black-hats, for example, can be further divided into various subgroups, such as basic coders, script kiddies, firebug hackers, legal black hackers and others.

In the criminal underworld, there are many other classifications and terms that designate a particular type of cybercrime perpetrators. The most commonly known [CHI 09] are wannabe lamer, cracker, ethical hacker, cyber-warrior, industrial spy, government agent, etc.

1.1.3. *Organization of perpetrators*

To prevent the unlimited growth of cybercrime, it is necessary to fight against it with the help of experts from different fields, such as psychology, criminal investigation, information security and similar, because only a sound knowledge of the problem and perpetrators can contribute to the successful fight against cybercrime. When referring to the knowledge of perpetrators, the author makes reference to a detailed analysis of their way of thinking, method of operation (*modus operandi*[17]), lifestyle, motives that lead

---

17 *Modus operandi*: a Latin phrase, roughly translated as "method of operation".

them to commit crimes and their organization. The research into and understanding of these topics, in particular, can be the greatest advantage in identifying the perpetrators. Today's offenders are most often organized into different interconnected groups. This ensures that the application of knowledge converges toward the common goal of the group; mostly this involves the unlawful acquisition of benefits or public visibility of actions. In the past, cybercriminals operated independently. They created their own hacking tools, invaded systems, created their own phishing pages that would send spam by themselves, steal bank account information, etc. Modern perpetrators are better organized, more connected and have advanced knowledge [WAL 08].

Several research studies have been conducted that analyzed the method of operation of crime groups in cyberspace. Figure 1.2 shows the organizational chart of a typical cybercrime group, which includes the following members [FIN 08]:

– The *boss* is the head of the organization. He operates as a business entrepreneur and does not commit the (cyber)crimes himself.

– Directly bereath him is the *underboss* acting as the second in command and managing the operation. In the case of cybercrime, he is the one that provides the Trojans for attacks and manages the Command and Control (C&C) of those Trojans.

– Beneath the underboss as lieutenants leading their own section of the operation, *campaign managers* lead their own attack campaigns. They use their own "affiliation networks" to perform the attacks and steal the data.

– The stolen data are sold by *resellers*. These resellers are not involved in the crimeware attacks, but trade the stolen data – similar to a "fence" dealing with stolen goods.

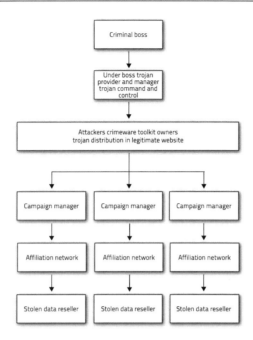

Figure 1.2. *Organizational chart of a cybercrime organization [FIN 08]*

The organizational structure of these groups is comparable to the organizational structure of the mafia [FIN 08, DOB 09]. The same situation that characterized the mafia in the past is now characteristic of the cybercrime perpetrators' subculture; an individual approach to cybercrime is replaced by the system of organizations that reflect the hierarchical structure typical of the mafia.

"With the transition of cybercrime from amateur hacker attacks to highly professional cybercrime business models, we see that the organizational structure of cybercriminals reflects the mentioned trend. Individual hackers operating independently or groups of hackers with common goals have been replaced by hierarchical cybercrime organizations were each cybercriminal has his own well-defined role and reward system. The current cybercrime organizations bear an uncanny resemblance to organized crime organization"

[FIN 08]. Since modern cybercrime is characterized by highly experienced criminal groups, it is necessary to choose an appropriate protection against attacks in order to ensure appropriate levels of security.

1.2. Tools for implementing attacks

Different groups use different tools or software. Some tools are widely known and used by perpetrators as well as professionals who use these tools in order to guarantee the security of information systems. Some of the most well-known tools are:

– Nmap (open source software for network research);

– Nessus (program for finding vulnerabilities in the network, which finds services and known problems; it consists of a Nessus client and server);

– Wire-shark (a tool for traffic analysis and tapping);

– Kismet (wireless network detector/packet sniffer);

– Cain & Abel (password cracking tool for Microsoft Windows);

– John the Ripper (password cracking program);

– the use of different key-loggers (small programs that run in the background of the operating system and record all the keys struck on a keyboard);

– the use of exploits[18];

– the use of botnets.

---

18 An exploit: a piece of software, a chunk of data or sequence of commands that takes advantage of a bug, glitch or vulnerability in the equipment, in order to cause unintended or unanticipated behavior to occur on the network, computer software, hardware or something electronic (usually computerized).

The offenders' subculture and the use of methods and techniques for carrying out attacks is extremely diversified; it includes a wide variety of individuals and groups with a variety of motives and purposes, and more recently, individuals from the cyber underworld seem to increasingly integrate into organized groups. With rare exceptions, their operation is focused on illicit acts, which harm individuals and organizations in different ways, and certain groups may also pose a threat to national security. When conducting detection and preventive activities related to cybercrime, experts fighting against it still have a great deal of work ahead of them.

1.3. System protection against attacks

Cybercrime is similar to classic crime. New security measures lead the perpetrators to search for new ways of committing these crimes [FUR 04]. The protection of ICT is a complex process. A computer must first be protected physically – it must be in a protected room. Recently, more and more mobile devices are being used and a lot more attention should be paid to them. These devices are normally left in our bags, cars and on the floor; but our lack of care can have serious implications. A mere moment of carelessness is enough for people to lose all their data. However, as we carry the data with us most of the time, we sometimes forget to be careful. Therefore, the idea that a man is the greatest threat to a computer system and to their own security still, and ever increasingly, holds true [BER 11a]. Greater care has to be awarded to the individuals' authorization to access sensitive data in the information system, the knowledge they have and what their motive could be, since this can reduce the number of attacks and keep instances of system abuse to a minimum. It is clear that employees have the greatest motive because they have direct access to the system. A further step in guaranteeing protection is to protect the communications and thus control the access. However, people are often reckless in doing so because they are over-reliant on passwords that are often weak, while access to such passwords by using social engineering and the inspection of records, trash, etc., is relatively easy. Cryptographic methods, which are used for encrypting in electronic commerce, are divided into symmetric and asymmetric cryptography. However, cryptography[19] does not help if the attacker gets the cryptographic key due to the user's recklessness, negligence or ignorance.

To reduce the impact of cybercrime and other forms of cyber victimization on the information systems of individuals, organizations or countries, the IC3 [IC3 10a] suggest the following:

– Take care when opening links in e-mails, especially from unknown URLs. This prevents installing Trojan programs, malware and phishing, thereby reducing the threat to computers and data stored on them.

– Be aware that the publication of private data provides possibilities for their abuse. Such data can be used to understand user's behavior and work methods, and allow the manipulation of users and the retrieval of their identity.

– Check the identity of the person who would like to obtain important information from you (phone verification, return message).

– Take care when installing add-ons and applications on computers and mobile devices. If users do not know the functions of add-ons and applications, they should not install them because some might open access into the system over the network, and thus enable the theft of personal and/or business data.

---

19 Cryptography: a science that deals with the study of procedures to protect the integrity, confidentiality and authenticity of data. Cryptographic methods are used in e-commerce for protection – data encryption (symmetric and asymmetric cryptography).

– Make sure you update antivirus software and firewall, and ensure their continuous operation.

– Passwords and pin codes must not be trusted to anyone. It is necessary to prevent the possibility of an unauthorized person getting access to them. It is recommended to take extra care when storing such data and respect the privacy when entering them.

– Change passwords regularly. They should be complex enough and should not consist of general facts (names, dates of birth and anniversaries).

– Use common sense when accessing cyberspace and connecting to it. Promotions, large lottery winnings, which request data from users, or money transfers, are usually fraudulent.

Education and training on the dangers of cybercrime has to become a part of everyday life at all levels of social life in order to have informed individuals who use the Internet thoughtfully and responsibly without fear of being abused. Some fear is useful, because it increases the user's care when working with a computer, and thus reduces the risk. It makes no sense to reduce fear too much because this can have the opposite effect [MES 03]. The author finds that there is a general lack of awareness around cybercrime and cyberlaw among people who frequently use ICT, both for business and private purposes. Users must be acquainted with the manifestations of cybercrime in order to reduce fear of it and to raise awareness of its existence.

1.4. Fear of cybercrime

One of the most commonly studied topics in criminology is the fear of crime [MES 06], so the knowledge of this phenomenon in the field of cybercrime is also essential. The perception of threat, and our awareness and fear of cyberspace are matters for an individual, but an understanding of this field is necessary due to research into and the development of guidelines for the safe use of cyberspace. In postmodern times, there is almost no social reflection that would not devote special (if not central) attention to the uncertainties and fears and anxiety emerging from them [KAN 05]. Users are almost constantly connected to and within cyberspace, since the technology – mobile devices, computers and the Internet – is available virtually everywhere. Researchers found that the fear of crime is usually higher than the actual level of crime in society [MES 08]. Despite a low level of abuse, many people are afraid to use credit cards in online shops, but in the real world they use it easily and also lose control of it; they are afraid of the misuse of data, even though cases of online credit card abuse or identity thefts in cyberspace are relatively rare compared to the ones in the real world. However, we might ask whether these examples are really rare, or whether they are just not appearing in the media. It can be observed very quickly that certain media-exposed cases create a higher level of fear than is proportional to the actual threat and possibility of victimization. Young [YOU 07] notes that mass media are spectacular places of exclusion: they bring order, justice and inclusion (news background) to the public, while intentionally highlighting errors, injustice and exclusion, and put these elements to the forefront. It is believed that this also applies to the perception of cybercrime, which often comes to effect as described by Cockcroft [COC 09]; news media probably represent the most pervasive way of informing people, since their real-time reporting and access to the general public often takes advantage of the possibility to provoke a surprise due to their sensationalist reporting. The level of fear that people have of crime depends on how much they are aware of the possible consequences. Mesko and Sifrer [MES 08] note that the fear of crime does not depend on the actual scope of crime. It thus depends on the individual's image of how the consequences of their actions in cyberspace might influence their lives. Various threats can induce fear in an individual towards any threats to their system and the consequences that come with it [BER 11]. This arises from a lack of knowledge in certain areas, which results from the fact that technology is nowadays accessible to everyone, and that work procedures are so simplified that the user can use devices and communication systems without any prior knowledge and therefore without understanding what is actually happening in cyberspace. Since users do not understand what happens, they also do not have an appropriate and relevant protection. The users thus help the perpetrators of cybercrime to abuse their systems or data, or contribute to their own victimization due to their ignorance or indifference. According to preliminary research and presented findings, the appropriate and responsible behavior of users in cyberspace represents the most effective protection and carries a smaller risk for an individual. The media, particularly the news media, in which a significant proportion of cybercrime reporting is concerned with the Internet content present on the World Wide Web, Facebook or communication via chain letters, use such content to produce sensationalist reporting. Such reporting often strongly influences the fear of cybercrime. Due to the media's contextually incomplete reporting, the public is not informed of the protection and the necessary measures for protecting individuals, but is rather discouraged from taking serious action. The media coverage often creates general opinions and uses myths about crime to justify social actions, which are based primarily on an emotional response to the reporting of criminal offenses. Measures, mainly repressive, are justified by citing expert opinions on crime, social supervisory practice, as well as existing and expected institutional and other responses to crime [MES 00]. More and more people are routinely using cyberspace. The use of e-commerce has also become extremely common. In this respect, business security is often mentioned, since the misuse of such systems can generate significant losses. Therefore, resources which are of a certain value for their owners and enable them to reduce the risk of exposure to threats are the focal point of security in the field of e-commerce [GRA 10].

D'Arcy *et al.* [D'AR 09] believe that in order to reduce unfounded fear of cybercrime, users should be informed about this phenomenon, which is why they propose the use of the following three security measures to reduce the threat and fear of cybercrime:

– increased user's awareness of potential threats;

– safety education;

– user's awareness of self-protection.

As determined by Bulgurcu *et al.* [BUL 10], different levels of threat awareness and knowledge of how to defend oneself against sources of threats in cyberspace are reflected in the behavior of an individual in cyberspace.

The awareness of potential threats in cyberspace and the fear of cybercrime depend on the users' knowledge of sources of threat and their perception of the threats that beset them when working in cyberspace. It should be noted that recent studies [PON 11] show a significant exposure to cybercrime and high costs associated with eliminating its consequences. In fact, the rate of cyberattacks is constantly increasing or the monitoring of these attacks is more systematic. The aforementioned study [PON 11] notes as much as a 44% increase in cyberattacks in comparison with the previous year. Therefore, situational awareness and risk-awareness is necessary in order to reduce the impact of threats on individuals and businesses. The results of research which demonstrates the use of a computer, the perception of sources of threat and the users' fear of cybercrime are presented below.

1.5. Investigation of cybercrime

Due to the sophisticated methods used to commit such offenses, the implementation and investigation of cybercrime has become more demanding and time-consuming. It is more difficult to detect perpetrators, and the police have to deal with the increasing amount of data and cases of abuse. To successfully investigate and punish acts of cybercrime, it is necessary to know and understand the operation of the perpetrators.

The main difference between paper documents and those in digital form is in the professional skills required for the review of digital data and evidence, the extent of stored digital data and the ease with which digital data can be damaged or destroyed [LOW 06]. Data in electronic form are an additional source of evidence that may constitute an offense in itself or can be an extension of an offense committed in the physical world [HIN 04]. This brings new challenges to law enforcement agencies in terms of seizing, eliminating and handling such information or evidence. The perpetrators leave behind digital traces that can lead to a dead end, and it is also easy to manipulate them in order to hamper the investigation. Therefore, forensic investigations of devices that store digital data are becoming an increasingly important element in criminal investigations both in the field of cybercrime and in other traditional forms of crime [MOH 03]. Law enforcement agencies are facing major problems and challenges posed by new methods of communication, the increasing sophistication and rapid advances in technology. The communication channels used by criminals can thus be conducted through many diverse technologies, such as public switched telephone networks, local or international providers of these technologies, and wireless and satellite connections. They can also pass through many countries with different time zones and jurisdictions. All of these options hinder law enforcement agencies in tracking and identifying perpetrators.

Perpetrators have many methods at their disposal for hiding their identity and reducing their chances of detection. Some methods require a fairly high level of knowledge and technical skill, but perpetrators can learn the majority of these methods with the assistance of sources that are freely available on the Internet. Some common methods include the use of fake or stolen personal data when registering with a certain Internet provider, the use of anonymous e-mails, the invasion of one or more servers that enable certain activities to be carried out, the use of anonymous servers that do not pass on information about the user (mainly IP addresses) and the falsification of information about the IP address, e-mail and Website. Today, the field of cybercrime is characterized by virtual locations, which enable perpetrators to migrate between them and thus avoid legal penalties and actions undertaken by law enforcement authorities [ZAV 07]. The Websites on which they carry out their unlawful activities (dissemination of child pornography, illegal sale of copyrighted works, etc.) are usually placed on servers in countries with inadequate laws, no international agreements and with less qualified law enforcement authorities. Such problematic areas mainly include South America, Africa and some less developed countries of Eastern Europe and the former Soviet Union.

In dealing with offenders and the investigation of cybercrime, it is observed that there is much talk about the losses caused by it; however, only a few articles and studies deal with its costs. Data regarding most losses are obtained on the basis of statistical surveys among companies or those affected, and only a few scientific publications in the past have considered the problem of calculating the actual costs that cybercrime poses at different levels in detail; at the level of an individual, an organization or a country.

1.6. Cost of cybercrime

Many studies and documents [PON 11, PON 12, UNO 10, ALP 11] have examined the costs and losses caused by cybercrime. Some works estimated the overall costs, others evaluated the costs of individual countries, while individual documents even assessed losses of certain organizations regardless of their size and technological development. In 2008, ENISA [ENI 08] assessed security economics and the internal markets and prepared an analysis based on the security economics of practical problems in network and information security that the European Union faces. They analyzed 15 policy proposals that should make an appropriate next step in tackling the problems.

Notwithstanding the above-mentioned research, none of them have presented a general model for calculating the cost of cybercrime until now. Therefore, the best experts in the field of cybercrime decided to prepare a model entitled "Measuring the Cost of Cybercrime" and published it in a paper authored by Anderson *et al.* [AND 12], whereby the introduction states: "We present what we believe to be the first systematic study of the costs of cybercrime. It was prepared in response to a request from the UK Ministry of Defense following skepticism that previous studies had hyped the problem. For each of the main categories of cybercrime we set out what is and is not known of the direct costs, indirect costs and defense costs – both to the UK and to the world as a whole". In this study, the authors carefully separated traditional crime that is now carried out in cyberspace (e.g. tax fraud or deception by selling products related to well-being and health improvement), and traditional crime in which the perpetrators' method of operation changed significantly due to the possibility of abuse in cyberspace (credit card fraud) and new types of crime that have been developed with the expansion of the Internet. They thus use the cyberspace platform for committing criminal offenses (use of botnets) that enable a crime to be committed indirectly. The costs are divided into direct and indirect costs, whereby direct costs or amounts are usually small, almost minimal, and do not cause severe harm to victims of cybercrime.

1.6.1. *Measuring the cost of cybercrime model*

Indirect costs and defense costs in the field of cybercrime are very high and significantly higher than classic crime. For example, in order to combat spam alone, produce spam software and provide education, billions of dollars are spent every year. The fact is that we, as a society, are very ineffective in the fight against cybercrime. Criminals, on the other hand, impose disproportionately high costs on the society. This mainly happens due to the global nature of cybercrime and strong external influences. Therefore, experts who prepared the above-mentioned model [AND 12] offer the following response: "As for the more direct question of what should be done, our figures suggest that we should spend less in anticipation of cybercrime (on antivirus, firewalls, etc.) and more in response – that is, on the prosaic business of hunting down cyber-criminals and throwing them in jail".

For a comprehensive understanding of the presented model entitled "Measuring the Cost of Cybercrime", the authors will, in addition to the aforementioned definitions of cybercrime, also consider the definition that the European Commission presented in its Communication entitled "Towards a general policy on the fight against cybercrime", which represents the agreed definition of cybercrime [ECO 07]. In practice, the term "cybercrime" is applied to three categories of criminal activity:

– traditional forms of crime such as fraud or forgery, though in a cybercrime context this relates specifically to crimes committed over electronic communication networks and information systems;

– the publication of illegal content over electronic media (i.e. child sexual abuse material or incitement to racial hatred);

– crimes unique to electronic networks, i.e. attacks against information systems, denial of service and hacking.

The model of costs' calculation, which relies on the following categories, had already been proposed in a Detica report [DET 11]:

– costs in anticipation of cybercrime, which include individual and organizational security measures (such as installing physical and virtual protection such as antiviral software), insurance costs and costs associated with gaining compliance to required IT standards (for example the Payment Card Industry Data Security Standard (PCI DSS));

– costs as a consequence of cybercrime, which take into account direct losses to individuals and companies (including business continuity and disaster recovery response costs), and indirect losses arising from reduced commercial exploitation of IP and opportunity costs through weakened competitiveness;

– costs in response to cybercrime, such as compensation payments to victims of identity theft, regulatory fines from industry bodies and indirect costs associated with legal or forensic issues;

– indirect costs associated with cybercrime, which include such factors as reputational damage to organizations, loss of confidence in cyber transactions by individuals and businesses, reduced public sector revenues and the expansion of the underground economy.

The Detica model uses the above-mentioned definitions in order to investigate the impact of cybercrime on the main affected groups: citizens, labor organizations and countries. In this context, the economic impact on each group is, or should be, taken into account.

The authors of the "Measuring the Cost of Cybercrime" model did not use this approach, as they believe "that the second heading includes both, direct and indirect costs" [AND 12], and that the third heading consists of direct costs in its entirety. In their model, the authors use a more straightforward approach which splits direct costs from indirect costs and which also includes the costs of security and the social and opportunity costs of reduced trust in online transactions.

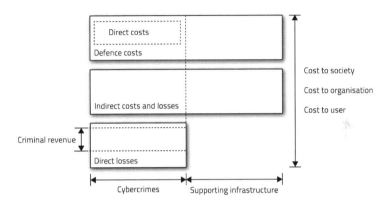

Figure 1.3. *Measuring the cost of cybercrime [AND 12]*

On the basis of the model's development and the simple and clear presentation of costs, the model defines the following categories of costs according to Anderson *et al.* [AND 12]:

– Criminal revenue is the monetary equivalent of the gross receipts from a crime and does not include any of the criminal's "lawful" business expenses.

– Direct loss is the monetary equivalent of losses, damage or other suffering felt by the victim as a consequence of a cybercrime. Examples of the direct losses include: money withdrawn from victim accounts, time and effort to reset account credentials (for both banks and consumers), distress suffered by victims, secondary costs of overdrawn accounts: deferred purchases, inconvenience of not having access to money when needed, lost attention and bandwidth caused by spam messages, even if they are not reacted to.

– Indirect costs and losses are the monetary equivalent of the losses and opportunity costs imposed on society by the fact that a certain cybercrime is carried out, no matter whether successful or not and independent of a specific instance of that cybercrime. Indirect costs generally cannot be attributed to individual victims. Examples of indirect losses include: loss of trust in online banking, leading to reduced revenues from electronic transaction fees, and higher costs for maintaining branch staff and cheque-clearing facilities, missed business opportunity for banks to communicate with their customers by e-mail, reduced uptake by citizens of electronic services as a result of lessened trust in online transactions and efforts to cleanup electronic devices infected with the malware for a spam sending botnet.

– Defense costs are the monetary equivalent of prevention efforts. They include direct defense costs, i.e. the cost of development, deployment and maintenance of prevention measures, as well as indirect defense costs, such as inconvenience and opportunity costs caused by the prevention measures. Examples of defense costs include security products, such as spam filters, antivirus and browser extensions to protect users; security services provided to individuals, such as training and awareness measures; security services provided to industry, such as Website "take-down" services, fraud detection, tracking and recuperation efforts; law enforcement; and the inconvenience of missing an important message falsely classified as spam.

The cost to society, an organization or user is the sum of direct losses, indirect losses and defense costs.

Indirect costs in the field of cybercrime are disproportionately high because the cost of security technologies, such as firewalls, spam filters and antivirus programs, can amount to a few hundred dollars per year. Therefore, those who are assessing the consequences of cybercrime and the authors who are preparing this kind of model are asking themselves: "Why does cybercrime carry such high indirect and defense costs? Many of the reasons have been explored in the security-economics literature:

there are externalities, asymmetric information and agency effects galore. Globalization undermines the incentives facing local police forces, while banks, merchants and service providers engage in liability shell games. We are also starting to understand the behavioral aspects: terrorist crimes are hyper-salient because the perpetrators go out of their way to be as annoying as possible, while most online crooks go out of their way to be invisible" [AND 12]. They continue: "The straightforward conclusion to draw on the basis of the comparative figures collected in this study is that we should perhaps spend less in anticipation of computer crime (on antivirus, firewalls, etc.) but we should certainly spend an awful lot more on catching and punishing the perpetrators".

This problem is also interesting from the point of view of the response to cybercrime. Apparently, the previous guidelines, instructions and directives to fight cybercrime have not led to an appropriate situation or a solution in this field. If we take a look at the other model, which was prepared for the calculation of operating costs of organizations being attacked from cyberspace, we can better understand the existing method of combating abuse and the potential need to find new organizational models and ways of combating the issue of cybercrime.

1.6.2. *Cost framework for cybercrime model*

During the same year, the Ponemon Institute [PON 12] carried out similar research and the preparation of a model for calculating operating costs of cyberattacks, which represents the cost model with the two separate cost streams used to measure the total cybercrime cost for organization (Figure 1.4). "These two cost streams pertain to internal security-related activities and the external consequences experienced by organizations after experiencing an attack" [PON 12].

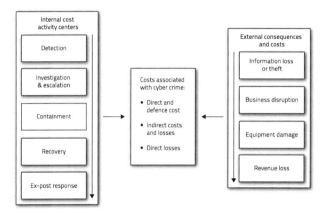

Figure 1.4. *Cost framework for cybercrime [PON 12]*

The study addresses the core process-related activities that drive a range of expenditures associated with a company's cyberattack. The five internal cost activity centers in the framework include [PON 12]:

– Detection: activities that enable an organization to reasonably detect and possibly deter cyberattacks or advanced threats. This includes allocated (overhead) costs of certain enabling technologies that enhance mitigation or early detection.

– Investigation and escalation: activities necessary to thoroughly uncover the source, scope and magnitude of one or more incidents. The escalation activity also includes the steps taken to organize an initial management response.

– Containment: activities that focus on stopping or lessening the severity of cyberattacks or advanced threats. These include shutting down high-risk attack vectors such as insecure applications or endpoints.

– Recovery: activities associated with repairing and remediating the organization's systems and core business processes. These include the restoration of damaged information assets and other IT (data center) assets.

– Ex-post response: activities to help the organization minimize potential future attacks. These include adding new enabling technologies and control systems.

As shown in Figure 1.4, costs, in addition to internal factors, also result from external factors and costs associated with the consequences of successful attacks on information assets outside the company. Thus, the four general cost activities associated with external consequences [PON 12] are the following:

– Cost of information loss or theft: loss or theft of sensitive and confidential information as a result of a cyberattack. Such information includes trade secrets, intellectual properties (including source code), customer information and employee records. This cost category also includes the cost of data breach notification in the event that personal information is wrongfully acquired.

– Cost of business disruption: the economic impact of downtime or unplanned outages that prevent the organization from meeting its data processing requirements.

– Cost of equipment damage: the cost to remediate equipment and other IT assets as a result of cyberattacks to information resources and critical infrastructure.

– Lost revenue: the loss of customers (churn) and other stakeholders because of system delays or shutdowns as a result of a cyberattack. To extrapolate this cost, we use a shadow costing method that relies on the "lifetime value" of an average customer as defined for each participating organization.

Even though Figure 1.4 does not show this directly, the costs of external attacks include the following attack types: "viruses, worms, Trojans; malware; botnets; web-based attacks; phishing and social engineering; malicious insiders (including stolen devices); malicious code (including SQL injection); and denial of services" [PON 12].

However, as attack techniques are constantly changing, improving and perfecting, it is necessary, for the actual calculation of costs, to include all elements, even if some are not included or explicitly mentioned in the presented models.

The models for calculating costs caused by cybercrime, which were presented or mentioned above, as well as other models, thus do not show the entire range of the problem. The main problem is the user's dependence on cyber infrastructure and their need for interacting with cyberspace. Protective mechanisms, if these are to be used in a comprehensive and therefore effective way, reduce the functionality and limit normal work. On the basis of the presented types of costs, the review of research regarding significant losses due to cybercrime, and the realities of modern cybercrime, we cannot but agree with the following statement made by Anderson *et al.* [AND 12]: "Indeed, the crooks are simply being rational: while terrorists try to be as annoying as possible, fraudsters are quite the opposite and try to minimize the probability that they will be the targets of effective enforcement action".

Do individuals, organizations and countries cope adequately with the problem of cybercrime and does invested time and money achieve its purpose? It can certainly be established that this is often not the case. So, in order to effectively cope with the ever increasing phenomenon of cybercrime and ever more aggressive attacks by modern cybercrime offenders, who mostly work internationally, it is necessary to ensure the quality of international cooperation within institutions and through relevant legal acts, and the implementation of the agreed and applicable international law in order to successfully prosecute crime, take the perpetrators to court and sentence them accordingly.

1.7. Laws and legal bodies

When entering cyberspace, users should be aware that they are entering a global space with no geographical boundaries. It is therefore important that they be subject to the laws and ethical values of many different cultures, societies and countries. Even though it is impossible to satisfy all the people at all times, complying with the laws of other countries and nationalities is an area where it is preferable to ask permission to carry out a certain action rather than to ask forgiveness later. When someone compromises our information system and commits a harmful or potentially criminal offense, it is very important to work together with law enforcement authorities to investigate and prosecute cases of attacks.

Effective cooperation and coordination between many different competent authorities and legal systems is undoubtedly the main challenge for law enforcement authorities or countries involved in the investigation of cybercrime.

1.7.1. *The Council of Europe Convention on Cybercrime*

The first step toward international cooperation and prosecution of cybercrime was the adoption of the Convention on Cybercrime [COC 01], hereinafter referred to as the Convention, drafted by the Council of Europe and signed by 34 countries in 2001 in Budapest. It entered into force on 1 July 2004 [UNI 04]. As of 28 October 2010, 30 states had signed, ratified and acceded to the Convention, while a further 16 states had signed the convention but not ratified it [COE 10]. The Convention was ratified by the following Member States of the Council of Europe: Albania, Armenia, Azerbaijan, Bosnia and Herzegovina, Bulgaria, Croatia, Cyprus, Denmark, Estonia, Finland, France, Germany, Hungary, Iceland, Italy, Latvia, Lithuania, Moldova, Montenegro, the Netherlands, Norway, Portugal,

Romania, Serbia, Slovakia, Slovenia, Spain, the former Yugoslav Republic of Macedonia and Ukraine, while among Non-Member States of the Council of Europe it was ratified only by the United States. The Convention was signed but not yet ratified by the following Member States of the Council of Europe: Austria, Belgium, Czech Republic, Georgia, Greece, Ireland, Liechtenstein, Luxembourg, Malta, Poland, Sweden, Switzerland and the United Kingdom. Among Non-Member States, the Convention was signed, but is not yet ratified by Canada, Japan and South Africa. Among Member States of the Council of Europe, the following countries still have to sign and ratify the Convention: Andorra, Monaco, Russia, San Marino and Turkey. It is more problematic if Russia, Japan, China, India and some other similar countries do not sign and ratify the Convention because attacks often come from these countries and prosecuting perpetrators is thus almost impossible.

After the aforementioned date, the Convention has been ratified only by the United Kingdom [LEY 11] during the visit of the US President in May 2011, when President Barack Obama and the UK Prime Minister David Cameron agreed to work more closely on cybersecurity.

Apart from the Convention, it is also necessary to mention the Additional Protocol to the Convention on Cybercrime, concerning the criminalization of acts of a racist and xenophobic nature committed through computer systems [COE 03], which extends and complements some of the elements of the Convention.

The goal of the Convention is thus to create a common policy of States Parties which would protect society against cybercrime, including the adoption of appropriate national legislation and fostering international cooperation. It defines criminal offenses involving copyright infringements, fraud connected with crime, child pornography and offenses related to network security. At the same time, the Convention also defines a number of procedural authorities, such as the search and interception of content on computer networks, and is contextually divided into the following [RUP 03]:

– Criminal offenses against the confidentiality, integrity and availability of computer data and systems, including:

- the intrusion into a computer system,

- the unlawful interception and interruption of data and systems,

- the misuse of devices.

– Crimes related to computers:

- computer forgery,

- computer fraud,

- offenses related to transferred content, among which offenses relating to child pornography undoubtedly stand out,

- offenses related to infringements of copyright and related rights.

States Parties to the Convention undertake that they will carry out the prosecution of all offenses defined in the second chapter of the Convention on their territory. The Convention also provides liability for attempting, aiding or abetting the aforementioned crimes, liability of legal persons and framework guidelines for the punishment of criminal offenses set out in the Convention. Its criminal and procedural provisions are divided into [RUP 03]:

– general provisions, which request States Parties to designate competent authorities and procedures for dealing with criminal offenses and to guarantee the respect for human rights and fundamental freedoms in accordance with current legislation and accepted international obligations in this area;

– provisions which define quick access to and disclosure of computer-stored data and are crucial particularly due to the characteristics of cyberspace;

– provisions relating to the request for, and investigation and seizure of computer-stored data;

– provisions regarding the collection of computer data in real time;

– provisions defining certain guidelines for determining jurisdiction.

From the point of view of criminal proceedings, a completely new set of specific methods and resources has to be provided for the purposes of prosecuting criminal offenses in cyberspace, while at the same time it is necessary to pay at least as much attention to the protective instruments that will effectively prevent their abuse [ZAV 07].

International cooperation covered by Chapter III of the Convention is crucial. Due to the anonymity and geographical vagueness of countries, law enforcement authorities are often faced with the limitations of their powers, which usually, in the absence of relevant international agreements, prevent them from effectively prosecuting and arresting cybercrime offenders. The provisions of the Convention are focused mainly on eliminating such boundaries in jurisdiction.

1.7.2. *Agreement on Trade-Related Aspects of Intellectual Property Rights*

The Agreement on Trade-Related Aspects of Intellectual Property Rights (TRIPS) [TRI 94] is an international agreement administered by the World Trade Organization (WTO) that sets minimum standards for different forms of intellectual property regulation as applied to nationals of other WTO Members [KIN 13]. It determines rules for the protection of intellectual property in a multilateral trade system and it is the first international instrument concerning the protection of intellectual property rights of individuals and sovereign nations. It includes WTO requirements for countries to control and regulate the legal aspects of intellectual property rights for the protection of intellectual property. The agreement covers the following areas [TRI 94]:

– The applicability of the basic principles of GATT 1994 and of relevant international intellectual property agreements or conventions.

– The provision of adequate standards and principles concerning the availability, scope and use of trade-related intellectual property rights.

– The provision of effective and appropriate means for the enforcement of trade-related intellectual property rights, taking into account differences in national legal systems.

– The provision of effective and expeditious procedures for the multilateral prevention and settlement of disputes between governments.

– Transitional arrangements aiming at the fullest participation in the results of the negotiations.

This document is an important contribution to the regulation of copyright and sets out the protection for software, music and video materials, and copyright of web pages, documents and other intellectual property related to cyberspace.

1.7.3. *Digital Millennium Copyright Act*

The Digital Millennium Copyright Act (DMCA) [DMC 98]) is a United States contribution to the topics of copyright law that implements two 1996 treaties of the World Intellectual Property Organization (WIPO). It criminalizes the production and dissemination of technology, devices or services intended to circumvent measures – digital rights management (DRM) that control access to copyrighted works. This Act has been drafted on the basis of Directive 95/46/EC of the European Union [DIR 95] and includes the following areas in the field of authorship:

– Title I, the "WIPO Copyright and Performances and Phonograms Treaties Implementation Act of 1998", implements the WIPO treaties.

– Title II, the "Online Copyright Infringement Liability Limitation Act", creates limitations on the liability of online service providers for copyright infringement when engaging in certain types of activities.

– Title III, the "Computer Maintenance Competition Assurance Act", creates an exemption for making a copy of a computer program by activating a computer for purposes of maintenance or repair.

– Title IV contains six miscellaneous provisions, relating to the functions of the Copyright Office, distance education, the exceptions in the Copyright Act for libraries and for making ephemeral recordings, "webcasting" of sound recordings on the Internet and the applicability of collective bargaining agreement obligations in the case of transfers of rights in motion pictures.

– Title V, the "Vessel Hull Design Protection Act", creates a new form of protection for the design of vessel hulls.

A complete understanding of any provision of the DMCA requires reference to the text of the legislation itself.

1.7.4. *United Nations Charter*

The Charter of the United Nations is the foundational treaty of the international organization called the United Nations [UNI 45]. Certain provisions deal with cybersecurity and information warfare, and include the use of IT by sovereign states for the implementation of organized and legally defined military operations, which take place in cyberspace in the modern world, and are considered as the basic legal acts for the supervision of operations described in the next section.

1.8. Cybercrime conclusion

Cybercrime has become a widespread phenomenon, which is emerging in numerous cases that cannot be classified as criminal offenses due to the vagueness of definitions, misunderstandings or incomplete legal acts. Cybercrime is thus a serious problem which modern society has to face. Because many users recklessly publish many items of their personal data online on a daily basis, they are faced with the risk that these data will be misused. If someone steals important information from a company, this can result in a huge loss of money and reputation.

There is practically no activity which does not use an electronic device connected to a computer network as one of the main tools for its completion, and this can consequently result in various cases of abuse described above. Therefore, in order to fight against cybercrime it is necessary to invest more effort and money, as well as to train more experts that would fight against the said problem even more eagerly.

Available funds must be directed toward the prosecution of offenders in a more reasonable manner, which would reduce the risk for users operating in cyberspace. With a better understanding of the cybercrime issue and greater knowledge of the possibilities of abuse, the users should be able to protect their IT infrastructure and restrict the publication of information in cyberspace, thus contributing their share to the protection of cyberspace and the reduction of abuse.

Since cybercrime today is no longer a game played by young people, but a profitable criminal affair, it is necessary to behave carefully and take into account both technical and user tips and techniques to reduce exposure and risks when participating in cyberspace. As the motives of perpetrators are very different, the aforementioned factors are, of course, difficult to avoid.

Above all, the international community should reach a consensus regarding what cybercrime actually is, establish an adequate legal basis, bring the perpetrators to justice, sentence them for their crimes and thus show that the fight against cybercrime is a fact and that crimes in cyberspace are not worth committing. It is also important for organizations to establish appropriate security policies, and to constantly educate and inform users who have to be aware of the risks. Undoubtedly, cyberwarfare[20] between different social groups, which poses additional risks, will become one of the major threats in the future.

Various groups, organizations and individual countries engaged in cyberwarfare are looking for ways to gain competitive advantage and ensure a successful survival. Therefore, this book also focuses on the power of information in cyberspace and the fight for gaining control over it. It is clear that apart from various groups and organizations, cyberwarfare is also used by individual countries, which play an offensive role to maintain or take leadership.

---

20 Cyberwarfare: offensive and defensive operations of (private and public) institutions or groups to acquire and/or use the information by using ICT in order to achieve superiority in the battle against the competition.

2

Cyberwarfare

"The U.S., Israel, China, and Iran are funding acts of hacker aggression, and the targets are as good as sitting ducks" [GRI 13]. This statement describes the current reality in cyberspace. The activity in which a certain country or organization attacks other countries or organizations has long been topical, but unnoticed by the general public, which gives us the feeling that these are just isolated cases and that individuals who point out the burning issues are too pessimistic regarding warfare in cyberspace. However, cyberwarfare occurs constantly, and many reports published in recent months even recount of a war between countries.

At the time of writing this book, McCaul [MCC 13] notes that nation states that wish to harm the United States "are sponsoring cyberespionage and are targeting the fastest route to the country's most sensitive information and critical infrastructure: wireless networks. Cyberwarfare is no longer an abstract threat to the homeland – it is happening now". Only a couple of days before the publication of the above statement, Constantin [CON 13] determined that "security researchers have identified an ongoing cyber-espionage campaign that compromised 59 computers belonging to government organizations, research institutes, think tanks, and private companies from 23 countries in the past 10 days". On the basis of this, we can find that 2013 marks the beginning of a new era in cyberspace – the age of cyberwars, which has supposedly originated from individual cases of cyberwarfare. Such cases usually do not affect normal users of cyberspace, but rather entities largely separated from the real world – countries' summits, military offices and global corporations – while the ordinary citizens should not feel the effects.

Written reports suggest that the time may have come when all of us who are dependent on information and communication technology (ICT) will have to think about cyberwarfare and its consequences, as Violino [VIO 13] states that an "unseen, all-out cyberwar on the U.S. has begun". Violino further notes that "there's a war going on, and it's raging here at home – not in the streets or the fields, but on the Internet. You can think of it as a war on the digital homeland. [...] A cyberwar has been brewing for at least the past year, and although you might view this battle as governments going head to head in a shadow fight, security experts say the battleground is shifting from government entities to the private sector, to civilian targets that provide many essential services to U.S. citizens".

If this is really happening, and there are no signs to indicate that it is not, a wave of cyberwarfare can also be expected in other areas of the informationally developed world, dependent on ICT and interconnected in cyberspace.

Politically, economically or ideologically motivated cybercrime is one of the most burning issues of contemporary society, which is still often underestimated. Broader social motivation, which is realized using ICT, is beyond individual interests and violates social norms, but is in most cases legal, undetectable, and in some cultural contexts even legitimate. ICT has exacerbated this situation, because its development has enabled a combination of different types of crimes to be carried out using the same techniques in a single cyberspace.

Offensive government action and related crime have always been different from classic crime, especially in terms of social harm and techniques used. Their merging into one of the most dangerous forms of crime for society – cybercrime – is thus even more problematic. The development of ICT and the Internet has paved the way for the development of various crimes that occur in cyberspace, including specific forms of warfare – i.e. cyberwarfare. Modern ICT is not only used for simplifying critical social and vital organizational functions, but also for the development of warfare techniques. This has deepened the problems associated with the detection, investigation and prosecution of state, business and ideologically motivated cybercrime. Because of the widespread availability of tools and knowledge, the techniques of achieving the objectives in cyberspace have become uncomplicated, and in most cases, comparable to other cybercrime. The main problem faced by competent authorities is the distinction between various forms of cybercrime, which can be achieved only on the basis of the identity of perpetrators and their motives. Determining the motivation is problematic, the anonymity, overall prevalence and access to cyberspace from a remote location, which are the main factors of modern ICT, allow the perpetrators to cleverly disguise their identity and the origin of attack.

As described in the previous section, cybercrime – like any other form of crime – cannot avoid the issue of legal regulation. This is why the legal definition of the cyberwarfare field currently remains incoherent, while the legal basis, with the exception of the Convention on Cybercrime [COC 01], is left to each individual country and their agreements on mutual assistance. Uncontrolled and global cyberspace, as well as the distance, impersonality and lack of understanding of its nature and legal constraints are the basic features of modern cyberwarfare, which threatens every country and its organizations.

Because of the scale of the problems associated with cyberwarfare, the authors strive to present its nature and provide possible responses to it. The disarray of the legal bases emphasizes the problem of detection and investigation of cybercrime and cyberwarfare related to global political, military and economic interests. On the basis of experience, state authorities and responsible persons of various organizations can learn how to respond properly or omit a response in crisis situations.

2.1. Information and cyberspace

In the ICT era, information and cyberspace have become inseparable concepts. Practically, everyone uses cyberspace on a daily basis in order to obtain information or share it with others. People use information and cyberspace as a basis for planning and performing their activities. As a result, people need the virtual world to perform their daily routines. Therefore, the permeation of modern ICT into the daily lives of individuals has become an increasingly common trend in the last 20 years. People have become completely dependent on it, in particular during the past few years.

The concept of cyberspace[1], which is linked to ICT, is the main reason for a new designation of modern society. The U.S. Department of Defense [EVA 09] defines cyberspace as a global domain in the information environment consisting of interrelated and interdependent IT networks. This includes the Internet, telecommunications networks and computer systems.

2.1.1. *Cyberspace and ICT*

As in any other social field, cyberspace, which represents a great social change, has also witnessed the development of theories that define the nature, meaning and impact of this

---

1 The word cyberspace was coined by William Gibson in his novel entitled *Neuromancer* in 1984, almost a decade before the formation of the World Wide Web [ZAV 05].

new spatial domain differently. There are two basic directions or theories that describe cyberspace: the liberal one refers to the advantages and benefits of cyberspace, while the realistic one describes the relationship between cyberspace and state power:

– The liberal direction indicates that cyberspace is a world in itself. Since the emergence of the Internet, when its users were still very limited, the liberalists had already recognized its revolutionary meaning. However, the liberal view is not uniform, but divided into two directions: utopian and pragmatic. Both consider cyberspace in an optimistic way, because they recognize its democratic and liberal capacities, and actors or users are seen as external observers, who are developing along with the process. The utopian view emphasizes the development of ICT, while pragmatists believe that the Internet is developing alongside intense international cooperation. It is believed that its control is necessary to supervise antisocial activities and the proper use of technology [ALB 06].

– The realistic direction believes that cyberspace is just like any other space. It places great importance on telecommunications, while it believes that changes in IT did not create new entities, but only compelled countries to adapt their (own) strategy. Cyberspace is understood as an extension of a battlefield and an economic market. When the question of earning related to cyberspace arose, (IT and cyber) warfare became inevitable. Cyberspace is, thus, not a source of new forms of power, but only an area in which the existing power transfers from the real world [MAN 10].

The practical use of ICT makes it clear that the global network, i.e. the Internet, created a new virtual space that coexists with the physical space. It is precisely because of the virtual nature of this "new space", i.e. cyberspace, that it has different characteristics in comparison with the real world. Following are the basic features that characterize cyberspace and distinguish it from other spaces [MAN 10]:

– The ability to mobilize users, including those who are difficult to include in the process by traditional methods.

– The ability to provide large amounts of non-regulated information at any time.

– The ability to shrink or eliminate geographical barriers and distance between users.

Information, speed, data flow and boundlessness represent the fundamental qualities of the new environment. Because of the advantages brought about by the modern ICT, its explosive integration into all social pores was inevitable. As soon as the network communications became more widely available, their use spread among all social strata. Berkowitz [BER 03] states that private industry took advantage of ICT for creating new earnings, international organized crime for more profit, political groups for achieving greater power and the army for creating new wars. Those who did not take advantage of these benefits are, according to the Darwinian Theory, lagging far behind the development, and if we summarize Alberts *et al.* [ALB 06], ICT became the DNA of the information age. The information age and its impact on society can be compared with the effects of the Industrial Revolution.

Apart from the benefits, for which it was adopted, every major change in society or in the mode of its operation also brings about negative consequences. This can be observed in the field of business and personal life that is interlaced with ICT. Eriksson and Giacomello [ERI 06] note that the principal intention of the development of the Internet was to simplify communication and not to ensure its safety. However, as ICT is now a key element of every critical infrastructure, from transport, power plants, communications and finance to administrative work and research, the security aspect is even more important. Western civilizations have spent a number of years establishing an information infrastructure that is mutually compatible and easy to use, but this has, according to Shackelford [SHA 09], created the Achilles heel of modern society. Large-scale vulnerability of information systems, opportunities for criminals to exploit this medium to reach their own, malicious objectives and the aggressive struggle for the control of information are, in addition to well-known benefits, also the fundamental threats of integration of ICT in the social sphere.

Safety is not the only problem associated with cyberspace. According to the authors' estimates, cyberspace, in addition to inadequate protection, also suffers from the following dilemmas:

– security issues are closely related to misunderstanding and fear of the use of modern ICT. Negligence or exaggerated fear of entering into such an environment can lead to under- or overestimation of an individual's security needs;

– issues related to inadequate supervision of cyberspace, its governance and legislative regulation. Norms represent a fundamental basis for regulating certain issues, while the absence of norms increases the opportunities and potentials for abuse;

– identification, investigation and prevention of security attacks in cyberspace. Various forms of crime in the physical environment use a variety of techniques to achieve specific goals. This is not the case in cyberspace, because the techniques of various types of cybercrime were unified. Inadequate legislation and a lacking understanding of it increase difficulties in tackling deviant phenomena in this spatial domain.

Because of ignorance and the poor knowledge of this space, inadequate legislation and the lack of support, it is difficult to achieve an adequate level of security, while an understanding of basic issues also needs to be obtained. In addition to traditional crime that moved into cyberspace, deviant behavior in this space also includes aggressive competition and fighting for information power or advantage.

2.1.2. *Information power and information conflict*

Cyberwarfare refers to politically motivated attacks on ICT for the purpose of penetrating the information systems of countries, organizations or groups, in particular, in order to commit sabotage and espionage. Cyberwarfare is understood as an analogy to the conventional battle, but this analogy is controversial due to its accuracy and political motivation.

Cyberwarfare, or the fight with or for information, has already developed through history, since the acquisition of information enables us to obtain a certain degree of power. Because of the exponential growth of information and the demand for it, the modern world is characterized by a particular type of power – information power. The importance of this kind of power is particularly evident in the field of politics, international relations and interorganizational competition, where socially responsible decisions, which are crucial for the success of the relevant entities, require accurate, timely, often confidential and, in particular, carefully protected information. These are often not owned by the person who needs and uses them. This is why Armistead [ARM 04] states that information is power and that the level of power depends on the use of information. Armistead also highlights the relationship between information and other forms of power. Unlike the past, when military, economic and diplomatic power represented the most important types of power, information in the 21st Century is becoming the most important factor for achieving domination in politics, while at the same time [ARM 04], it is also a force multiplier, a tool for decision making, aggressive campaigning and much more.

It is extremely difficult to define and categorize information power precisely because of these properties, as it interferes with military, political, economic and social power sources and, in some cases, reduces or increases their importance. In order for the information power[2] to be useful, it must be understood as such; if it is used improperly, it can cause harm. The power of information is extremely transferable [IOC 11], and besides that property, which represents the basis for personal, organizational, national and global development, and consequently success, it is becoming increasingly important. When considering information power, there is a paradox. Information power can have an important impact, which is why everyone would like to have it. However, information power is untamable, as information in modern society cannot be controlled, monitored, regulated or restricted. When possessing such power, doubts are raised, especially at the state level, where history has even witnessed the exploitation of information power. In the past, it was mainly authorities and the chosen few who maintained their power over the people with the assistance of the information they possessed. Immense advances in technology, computer and telecommunications sectors over the last decade caused the end of this monopoly and power over information. Apart from that, the merging of these formerly distinct sectors into a united field of ICT enabled the use of information on a much larger scale. In reality, authorities can no longer control information, as it is no longer limited to the source or mode of transmission. Therefore, Armistead [ARM 04] raises the question: "If they cannot control the information, can they still control the power?"

---

2 Information power: with the possession of information, we possess a certain degree of power. Because of the exponential growth of information quantity and the demand for it, it is possible to talk about information power. The importance of such power is particularly evident in the field of politics, international relations and interorganizational rivalry.

In the modern world, interconnected in cyberspace, information power is difficult to obtain and even more difficult to maintain or control. For this reason, warfare between opponents aimed at obtaining information power is present at all times, everywhere. The main purpose of this engagement is to achieve information dominance or superiority over the opponent. From fighting for information and power related to it, a new type of conflict has developed: information conflict. In the past, the world has experienced mainly political, economic and military conflicts, while the information age and the use of ICT have changed the classification of conflicts. Fight for information has become so constant, aggressive and widespread that one can speak of a new type or level of conflict.

An information conflict is often an obvious, open conflict, which can lead to serious consequences, such as an economic and military conflict [BAS 10]. Information conflicts can usually be found in the field of information, computer technology and computer networks, so these conflicts do not have the same degree of hostility as military conflicts. However, cyberwarfare encompasses attacks, defense and warfare, and can disable the national critical infrastructure, reduce military capability and curtail the government's ability to control and manage the state. Temporary effects, which can be caused by such actions, are similar to a military conflict; hence, the level of tensions in an information conflict is certainly greater than in an economic conflict. The information conflict provides an alternative to kinetic war when mutual conflict exceeds the first and second degrees. It represents a serious and dramatic conflict, which does not directly cover physical damage.

The information conflict is carried out by applying the techniques and methods of cyberwarfare, and is very different from the techniques used in the execution of the remaining three levels of conflict. Since the nature of the information conflict is almost more similar to classical cybercrime than to traditional warfare, the problems of defining and identifying cyberwarfare are even more pressing.

2.2. Understanding cyberwarfare

Cyberwarfare, which is carried out with the assistance of modern ICT, certainly falls within the scope of cybercrime in cases where information is obtained and used in violation of the laws and moral norms. In practice, the categorization of this contemporary threat is not that straightforward. Cybercrime attracted a lot of attention, especially with respect to the adoption of security policies and legislation, among law enforcement authorities and in the private sphere, while in the sphere of military bureaucracy, it is placed within the framework of cyberfighting, information operations, cyberterrorism and cyberwarfare. In professional circles, which deal with the use of ICT, the threats are named specifically, with a focus on attacks on computer networks, faults, disturbances and the use of information systems [ERI 06]. The understanding of cyberwarfare and crime related to it thus depends on the sphere, professional orientation and objectives of experts who define this concept. However, due to the nature of its development in the past, cyberwarfare is still imbued with a military sense.

In addition to military-related conflicts, the modern understanding of the phenomenon of cyberwarfare covers a wide range of social issues: economic, political, criminal, security and civil. Siroli [SIR 06] sees cyberwarfare not only as activities aimed at achieving dominance or advantage by influencing the opponent's information, information processes, information systems and computer networks, but also as a safeguard and protection of their own IT infrastructure. Cyberwarfare is composed of activities with the purpose to disavow, damage or destroy the opponent's sources of information, and it includes both attack and defense activities, which often overlap. Taylor et al. [TAY 06] define cyberwarfare as the protection, abuse, damage, destruction or disabling of information or their resources in order to achieve an advantage or victory over an opponent. Joyner and Lotrionte [JOY 01] believe that cyberwarfare is an information activity used at the time of crisis or conflict in order to achieve set objectives. Joint Chief of Staff (JCS), an advisory body that operates under the auspices of the U.S. Department of Defense, defines cyberwarfare as activities designed to achieve information superiority by affecting the opponent's information, information-based processes, information systems and computer networks, and the protection and defense of their own information, information-based processes, information systems and computer networks[3] [BET 06]. The aim of these activities is to use cyberspace to carry out attacks against personnel, objects or equipment in order to disable, damage, neutralize or destruct the capabilities of the opponent, while protecting their own. The primary purpose is to disable or disavow the freedom of the opponent in cyberspace [ALE 11].

In the United Kingdom, the term "information operations"[4], which indicates that the area of cyberwarfare is understood merely as a subcategory or support to conventional warfare, is often used instead of cyberwarfare. Information operations, as defined in JWP 3-80[5], are coordinated activities aimed at influencing the opponent or potential adversaries, as support for political and military interests by undermining their will, cohesion and decision-making skills, so that one influences their information, information-based processes and systems, but at the same time covers the protection of their own abilities and decision-making processes [BET 06].

---

3 Joint Chiefs of Staff Instruction No. 3210.0, Information Warfare.
4 Information operations: coordinated activities as a support for political and military interests with the intention to impact opponents or potential adversaries by undermining their will, cohesion and decision-making skills, while also protecting one's own abilities and decision-making processes.
5 Joint Warfare Publication 3–80, Information Operations [JWP 02].

The diversity of these definitions makes it clear that the path toward a general consensus on what is or is not covered by the emergence of information warfare is still long. As in all other fields of crime, and especially in the ever-evolving ICT, the field of cyberwarfare is also witnessing delays in the understanding and knowledge of the nature of perpetrators' operations and their techniques. If we take a look at the definition [SEA 10], which stipulates that "cyberwarfare is an Internet-based conflict involving politically motivated attacks on information and information systems" and that "cyberwarfare attacks can disable official Websites and networks, disrupt or disable essential services, steal or alter classified data and cripple financial systems – among many other possibilities", we could observe that the political motivation of groups, which carry out attacks, is one of the main factors leading to an attack on the "enemy". Cyberwarfare is, therefore, the result of merging the military and organizational objectives of a country with ICT and is basically related to the acquisition and/or use of the information with its assistance. The information is part of the information system involved in cyberspace, which is the object or tool of cyberwarfare, carried out through cyberattacks. An attack most often includes violations of laws, policies or regulations within the local or global environment, which is why cyberwarfare (often, but not always) falls within the scope of cybercrime [JUR 08]. With regard to this, the author suggests the following definition of modern cyberwarfare:

> Cyberwarfare is an offensive and defensive operation of (private and public) institutions or groups to obtain and/or use the information with the assistance of ICT in order to achieve superiority in the battle with the competition.

The desire of those who carry out cyberwarfare is to protect their own information against misuse, damage and destruction or to prevent the accessibility of data, while at the same time seeking to abuse, damage and destroy the data of the opponent and block their information system so that they cannot access their own information.

2.2.1. *The nature of cyberwarfare*

Because of its specific nature, which is determined by "war/combat" and "country/organization", cyberwarfare is taken out of the context of classic cybercrime. In an interview for the O'Reilly Website [SLO 10], Jeffrey Carr, the author of the book entitled *Inside CyberWarfare*, compared cyberwarfare with the invention of the revolver, which has revolutionized warfare. And this is exactly what is supposed to be happening with cyberwarfare by the occurrence of ICT. He also believes that cyberwarfare makes it possible to achieve a balance between unequal opponents. This is true due to two factors: the current vulnerability of the Internet and the involvement of military forces in both the local and the global network. The problem of cyberwarfare is not only related to the understanding and definition of the phenomenon, but also to its implications and dimensions. Illegal interference of state authorities and services in electronic devices, computer systems, networks and means of communication that fall within the scope of cyberwarfare, are nothing else but an act of state cybercrime. Here, we can actually talk about state crimes[6].

The advantage and superiority are the virtues of those who develop a certain technology first. The information revolution, together with globalization, transnational economics and access to communication and information of all types, offered individuals, companies and countries many new opportunities to obtain power. Any attempt to compete without the use of modern ICT would cause a major setback, as no organization could currently compete without the use of ICT. The lack of competitiveness brings about financial

---

6 State crimes: crimes carried out by the state to achieve its objectives.

loss and failure. Even the army would find it difficult to plan and coordinate operations without the use of ICT, which would result in lagging behind those who use modern technology. Fritz [FRI 08] argues that the benefits offered by technological dependence outweigh the risks. Aside from this, it is impossible for the country to establish an appropriate defense against cyberattacks, if it does not master the techniques of cyberwarfare.

The expansion and development of cyberwarfare was not only enabled by the high degree of dependence of business and state structures on ICT, but it was also made possible by the common forms of vulnerabilities that arose in information systems. In any case, opportunities or possibilities posed by these types of vulnerabilities increase the likelihood of an attack and the exploitation of security gaps, as modern ICT is anything but safe. Microsoft, the world's leading computer company, regularly analyzes and publishes reports on the vulnerabilities of their software, and at the same time, estimates weaknesses of programs of other manufacturers. The Microsoft Vulnerability Research has been running since 2008 and in the last year alone (from July 2010 to June 2011) as many as 109 types of vulnerabilities were detected in the software of 38 other manufacturers (these included WordPress, Google Picasa, Facebook and Safari tools), wherein more than 90% of the detected types of vulnerabilities were critical [NAR 11]. The combination of such forms of vulnerabilities and errors in software or users' negligence immensely facilitates the work of cyberwarriors.

Given the intense migration of crime in to cyberspace, the flood of information, mass forms of vulnerability, skilled offenders, intensive and expansive motivation and dependence on ICT, the transfer of information conflict into cyberspace is no longer a question but a fact. Knowing and developing techniques of cyberwarfare is essential to the successful operation of national and organizational structures and their defense against hostile intrusions into information systems.

2.2.2. *Types and techniques of cyberwarfare*

Using the techniques of cyberwarfare at the state level is usually aimed at obtaining information on the economic, political, cultural and military situations in another country – the target – or for specific offensive or defensive operations in cyberspace. In the first case, countries most often achieve the objectives through espionage, and in the second case, these are carried out through actions in cyberspace that are similar to military activities. However, cyberwarfare does not fall only within the competence of states, but is also used by corporations or those organizations, which need information for which they do not have authorized access for their survival, development and competition. New guidelines and needs for information, as well as knowledge related to it, will be increasingly dictated by aggressive competition and organizations lagging behind.

As an offensive activity, cyberwarfare consists of the following six components [TAY 06]:

– Psychological operations, which impact the mental state of an opponent (propaganda or dissemination of information to influence the decision making of people, whereby the Internet is a great tool for achieving this).

– Electronic warfare, which includes disabling of access to information needed by the opponent (usually carried out by terrorists, hacktivists[7] and countries).

---

7 Hacktivism: illegal political or ideological action in cyberspace (linking activism with hacking), such as movements related to anti-globalization, animal rights, workers' rights, movements against wars, environmental changes, piracy organizations, etc. (e.g. the Anonymous group).

– Military deception, which is similar to the one in traditional forms of warfare, whereby the opponent is misled regarding actual military capability.

– Physical cyberwarfare, which includes physical attacks on information systems.

– Protection measures to protect information system; the aim is to have a system that cannot be disabled by the opponent.

– Information attack[8], which covers the abuse, use or destruction of information.

An offensive information operation involves the collection of confidential information, unauthorized access to information systems, creating security loopholes in it, the modification or destruction of data and disabling or destroying an information system [JOY 01], whereas this kind of information "fighting" has the following two fundamental forms [JUR 08]:

– disinformation or deceiving the opponent and attack on the computer network;

– disruption or destruction of the opponent's information.

Cyberwarfare involves exploiting security loopholes in security systems, and this is why the information system is the main target of cyberwarriors. The wide availability of tools for carrying out an attack on a system is a fundamental issue connected with the existence and expansion of cyberwarfare and cybercrime, and their prevention. The first electronic bulletin board for hackers, which allowed a rapid exchange of hacker tactics and software[9], appeared around 1980 [KNA 06]. The basic tools for carrying out cyberattacks

---

8 Information attack: an attempt of unauthorized access to information, the unauthorized use, misuse and/or destruction of information.

9 Interpol estimates that about 30,000 websites enable the possibility of an automatic transmission of hacking tools and software suitable for intrusions to information systems and information misuse [SHA 10].

by cyberwarriors involve the same instruments that were used and developed by hackers (computers, communication devices, mobile phones, software, etc.). The method for committing cyberattacks and the technique used for this purpose depend largely on the type of perpetrator, their purpose and motive.

In addition to the general availability of tools on the Internet, the easily accessible education in the field of security and the methods for entering the protected ICT can also be observed frequently. Anyone who inquires about the techniques, methods and conditions for operating in cyberspace can find all the information and detailed training materials on various Websites. Information on the functioning of cyberspace, as well as tools that allow the misuse of this space, are available to everyone, which means that anyone who wishes to do so can learn cyberwarfare techniques. To facilitate readers' research into this topic, the authors present a list of basic methods for conducting cyberwarfare (both in terms of defense and attack), which include the following [JOY 01]

– Sniffer[10] (inserted into the system from a remote location to collect information about user names and passwords of the user).

– Trojan horse[11] (can be installed on the network system to enable the system management).

– Backdoor[12] (a security loophole through which one gains unauthorized access and control over the system).

---

10 Sniffer: spyware delivered to the system from a remote location, which collects user information (user names, passwords, banking information, etc.).

11 Trojan horse: malware placed in the information system through which we can manage the system without authorization.

12 Backdoor: security gap through which one gains unauthorized access and control over the system.

– Logic bomb (a malicious program that is activated under specified conditions).

– Video morphing (presenting news that cannot be separated from the original form).

– (D)DOS attack[13] (an attack on critical infrastructure by overloading the system with a large amount of requirements that may prevent the exchange of data between the systems of critical response).

– Botnet attack (reciprocal attack of infected computers (i.e. bots) over the Internet at the target information system).

– Computer virus or worm[14] (can travel over computer systems and, e.g., destroy/change data, and cause a breakdown or unavailability of the system).

– Information block (can prevent the transmission of data to or from a certain system in the area of a certain country).

– Spam (unwanted e-mails/harassment by e-mail: it can overflow the e-mail and thus prevent data from being transferred at the operational level).

– IP spoofing[15] (obtaining confidential military information under the pretense of an authorized command).

In addition to the aforementioned general techniques implemented by the application of basic tools and methods, Darnton [DAR 06] also lists some more specific techniques:

– theft and disclosure of confidential information;

– software traps on public networks;

---

13 Denial-of-Service attack: attack on the server connected to the Internet, with many access requests, in order to slow down, stop or disable the server.
14 Computer virus or worm: malicious code that is transmitted between computer systems and changes/destroys data, and causes damage or unavailability of the system.
15 Spoofing: a technique of manipulating IP addresses or e-mails to obtain unauthorized access to the information system.

– diversion of financial flows or damage/blocking of access to bank data;

– mass attacks on communications services (mass dialing attacks);

– electronic takeover of television and radio stations;

– change of formulas or information in health care;

– damage or interruption of state military command and control infrastructure;

– manipulation or damage of civilian infrastructure (energy, transport, finance, etc.).

Cyberwarfare methods and techniques used for committing cybercrime are usually based on a previously unauthorized access to an information system, which we want to compromise or misuse. Thefts, unauthorized disclosures or prohibited uses of information are among the most frequent objectives of cyberwarfare, which are achieved by attacking and damaging ICT. With regard to the attack on the system, two main techniques can be observed:

– Delivery: for the purposes of delivery, perpetrators use a variety of techniques, such as spam, Websites infected with viruses, the distribution of malicious programs through attachments to e-mails or the transmission of (often free) applications from public domains in cyberspace.

– Deployment: perpetrators use various strategies for the purposes of deployment. First, they try to hide the malicious program in the best possible way, which is achieved by turning off system notifications and warnings produced by antivirus programs, updating antivirus software, etc. Apart from that, modern malware guarantees its existence and ownership of the system by destroying other malicious software.

In terms of effects that can be caused by such techniques, we must always keep in mind that cyberwarfare is a weapon of mass disturbance and not a weapon of mass destruction [BER 03]. Web links that enable the perpetrators to deliver malicious software (malware) and gain unauthorized access to target systems are often used for carrying out information attacks and intrusion. As stated by the SANS Institute [SAN 07][16], this equipment most often consists of "key-loggers", i.e. applications that spy on user activities and transmit collected data to a remote location. Wireless Internet connections are also often used for intrusions and attacks on information systems for the purposes of espionage. In this context, it is important to note that the Internet is used by 34% of the world's population [INT 12], or approximately 2.4 billion users. Among these, there are millions of people who take advantage of Internet capabilities for malicious actions. For example, a lot of tools for committing cyberwarfare spread through e-mail. E-mails most frequently include various forms of computer fraud (such as phishing[17] and pharming[18]) and transfer spyware (e.g. key-loggers, Trojan horses, viruses, worms and malware), which collect confidential information from the user and send it to common servers or take control of the computer, which becomes a bot[19]. Given that spam represents such a large percentage of e-mails, the possibilities of cyberwarriors are unlimited, and anyone can become their victim.

The theft of business or private confidential information is much easier and faster when applying adequate knowledge and IT than spying in its physical form. Also, ICT is extremely widespread in the business sphere so knowledge of

---

16 SANS Institute: a private U.S. company specialized in education on Internet safety.

17 Phishing: a form of online fraud where one acquires personal or other necessary information from the user by masquerading as a trustworthy entity.

18 Pharming: a form of online fraud in which malicious software is installed on a computer system or server to redirect the user to a bogus website that tries to obtain their personal information.

19 Bot: a target machine that is infected by malware and becomes part of a botnet.

its operation is of general interest, since it is useful in all fields, irrespective of which field a certain spy works on. Unlike conventional spies, hackers who break into a computer system do not need to know much about the organization from which they want to obtain information. The work of hackers is certainly facilitated by mistakes in ICT systems and the negligence of employees who should take care of the appropriate system security. The techniques of cyberwarriors[20] are certainly diverse and adapted to the complexity, knowledge and type of endangered environment.

The highest level of threat or vulnerability can be observed in the following critical infrastructure [SIR 06]:

– Information and communication: apart from natural disasters, systems failures and their instability due to the complexity of the Internet represent a major threat; these also include intentional damage and malicious intrusions.

– Power supply: the vulnerability of this sector has increased due to an ever greater dependence on ICT and intertwined information systems (e.g. SCADA[21] systems, which control and monitor the overall infrastructure of energy operators and represent serious danger and high risk from the cyber point of view).

– Banking and finance: due to their high dependence on ICT, certain institutions are often subject to theft and counterfeiting. The employees represent the greatest threat because they exploit authorized access to steal confidential information. The desire to preserve business reputation and goodwill represents an additional problem, which often makes organizations of this type seem non-transparent, and which makes it even more difficult to detect threats and protect systems.

---

20 Cyberwarriors: people who use methods and techniques of cyberwarfare.
21 SCADA: Supervisory Control and Data Acquisition. Control systems that are usually used for industrial control systems.

– Physical distribution: due to its dependence on ICT, the transport sector is also subject to cyber threats, especially in terms of communications and management. Air transport, which is completely dependent on electronic systems, is particularly exposed.

– Supplying people with urgent necessities of life: the vulnerability of this sector is related to the dependence on SCADA systems, e.g. water, electricity and gas supply. Such a high level of vulnerability also occurs in the field of communications systems for emergency response services, government information systems and military information assets.

Security vulnerabilities that are exploited by cyberwarriors are also very dependent on the current political situation in a country, which impacts the organizational climate and structure. Cyber-Ark, a company dedicated to providing information security, conducted a survey among 600 employees in the United Kingdom, the United States and the Netherlands [FUL 09], in order to determine whether the financial and economic crises are affecting the working relations of people, their ethics and information security. The results showed that there were significant increases in industrial espionage and the theft of data, especially among employees afraid of losing their jobs, but not so much among hackers. Even the hacking community believes that the guidelines used in the global economy are creating new opportunities for them. The reduction of workforces has led to the outsourcing of certain functions in organizations, which further endangers the safety of cyberspace and information related to it. On the one hand, fewer employees who would be responsible for maintaining comprehensive information security result in the increased vulnerability of companies and leave more room for errors, while on the other hand, there are a lower number of people who have full access to ICT.

2.3. Perpetrators and victims of cyberwarfare

In the study of cyberwarfare, perpetrators can be victims at the same time. The target of cyberwarfare can be any country, organization or individual, which can also be the victim of other entities (for interstate, interorganizational and interpersonal cyberwarfare) at the same time. At the national level, it is difficult to talk about the most vulnerable points; however, critical infrastructure[22] is undoubtedly of vital importance for those who hold and need it, as well as for those who want to harm the opponent. As cyberwarfare does not have a typical front line, any ICT-supported system can represent a potential target: from oil, gas and power plants to fixed line networks, mobile phone networks, banking systems, insurance systems, water reservoirs, government offices, public administration, airports and finally individual users, who use ICT at home. Thus, business data theft cannot be avoided by any organization, even in the private sector, but some are more vulnerable to this type of crime, most often because they hold data that are of greater value to the recipient or to the person that manages to obtain them.

It is often mentioned (e.g. [CYB 11]) that the attack on Estonia was the first example of a cyberattack on a specific authority. The attack on Estonia's systems began in April 2006 with the flood of information on key government Websites, especially on the Websites of the president of the country, its government and parliament. One of these floods of data blocked the parliamentary e-mail system. The attack included about a million botnet computers in the United States and Asia, which flooded Estonian Websites with enormous amounts of data. The attacks were allegedly

---

22 Critical infrastructure: information networks and systems that have key positions in contemporary society, which the society is largely dependent on. For example, water, electricity and gas supply, telecommunications, emergency services, information services, transport and distribution, banking, finances, military and police operations.

planned online, and attackers communicated through the Russian-speaking chat rooms and forums.

This is not an isolated example, as many attacks on and intrusions into government and economic systems have already occurred. In this context, the victims of such attacks and targets of cyberwarriors can most often be found in the U.S. information points, which often became the target of malicious state or corporate sponsored spies and attackers due to their dependency on technology, advances in development and innovation, and military superiority. Recently, such attacks – some of which are described at the end of this chapter – have been happening almost constantly and they also became known to the public, e.g. the United States [LET 11], Israel [RAY 11] and China [PAU 11]. Many examples of Chinese espionage in the United States were discovered between 1995 and 2008. These activities were primarily focused on aircraft, spacecraft and marine structures, as well as on computer industry, the production of nuclear weapons, allied campaigns, etc. The perpetrators of espionage used all the information, including that collected through OSINT[23], which were acquired through a decentralized network of students, businessmen, scientists, diplomats and other citizens of China, who were mostly legitimate residents in the target country [FRI 08].

Great Britain was also unable to avoid Chinese attacks. In 2007, Jonathan Evans, the director of MI5, the British security service, sent directors of the 300 largest UK companies a letter in which he warned them that they are targets of cyberattacks performed by Chinese intelligence services. He was convinced that the attackers came from Chinese state organizations. The Chinese government was supposed to monitor large construction and oil companies, as well as law firms and other companies that do business with

---

23 Open-source intelligence (OSINT) is intelligence collected from publicly available sources.

China or manage strategically important information. He believed that the Chinese government hackers use specially designed Trojan horses for espionage[24], which is why he sent digital checksums of these programs and the IP addresses of servers from which they had carried out attacks to the representatives of companies. This was the first time that a representative of Great Britain officially accused China of electronic espionage [KOV 07], which demonstrates that no country or organization is safe from political cybercrime, including those who do business or otherwise cooperate with the perpetrator.

2.4. Committing cyberwarfare

Countries have acted as cyberwarriors for many years. Since the beginning of its development, ICT has been used in their military structure and, in addition to that, countries have consistently performed psychological information operations to maintain power and control over society. Similar activities are continuing even today; however, the redistribution of power, new conflicts and the dissemination of ICT have changed the achievement of their goals. Just like the perpetrators of classic cybercrime, countries are also taking advantage of modern ICT in gaining their foreign policy interests, disseminating propaganda (influencing the mindset of the people) and achieving military objectives. Espionage, propaganda activities and warfare are the fundamental areas related to cyberwarfare techniques.

2.4.1. *Espionage*

Countries are increasingly tightening their legislation on cybercrime and are trying to limit and prevent such kinds of actions by individuals and civil society organizations as

---

24 Espionage: a form of intelligence that involves penetration in areas where confidential information is stored.

much as possible, while at the same time the opposite tendency can also be observed, with countries extending the field of intervention and intrusion in communication and computer systems. They are creating immense systems for controlling all means of communication and increasingly training their personnel for illegal interventions in the computer and communications systems of individuals, corporations, government bodies and institutions. Since information is a highly sought-after commodity nowadays and the struggle for fresh and relevant information is becoming global, national cybercrime remains unpunished and is permitted by the international political public [DOB 09]. A typical example of this is Echelon[25], from which the United States has tangible benefits, as it uses it to supervise competitive economic information with a view to exploit it in an unjustified way and to the detriment of other countries in order to enhance the performance of the U.S. economy. In 2001, the European Commission in its final report for that year officially confirmed, for the first time, the existence of this spy network, which uses software tools that filter the intercepted data and searches for relevant information for the client.

In addition to electronic spying systems, the civil infrastructure and commercial sphere are also used to obtain confidential information necessary for cyberwarfare. Google recently confirmed that they have repeatedly handed over data on the provision of their services to European users to the U.S. intelligence services, despite the fact that the data were stored only on servers in Europe and not in the United States. The same was also confirmed by Microsoft, which handed over data regarding Office 365 users. Microsoft and Google were forced to hand over the data due to the

---

25 Echelon is a term associated with a global network of computers that automatically search through millions of intercepted messages for pre-programmed keywords or fax, telex and e-mail addresses. Every word of every message in the frequencies and channels selected at a station is automatically searched [FED 13].

American antiterrorism legislation, the Patriot Act, which binds U.S. companies to hand over all the required information, regardless of where the data are located. In doing so, they have consciously violated European provisions on the protection of personal data, which require the consent of an individual before the handing over of their data to third parties (foreign governments). A similar situation also occurred in relation to Facebook, as a disclosed confidential document[26] reveals that Facebook, at the request of government services, provides all data about users, including their private conversations, past activities and personal data of their friends [MAN 11].

By using the described methods, countries are trying to provide data and information for the purposes of national security, as well as for the needs of private economic spheres. Thus, countries are helping companies by giving them strategically important economic information. The Echelon spy system is still primarily designed to gather military and political data, but the advantage of power in the military and political spheres is incomplete if one does not also have economic domination. Such systems are usually part of intelligence activities[27] or are intended for the collection of information in a way that is characteristic of covert operations conducted by law enforcement agencies. When collecting data and implementing attack or defense in the military sphere, a certain country can also use other cyberspace techniques that are more characteristic of warfare than intelligence operations.

---

26 Available at: http://www.eff.org/files/filenode/social_network/Facebook 2010_SN_LEG-DOJ.PDF
27 Intelligence activities: public or covert gathering of data by intelligence agencies, and their analysis and interpretation through the implementation of counter-intelligence activities.

2.4.2. Active warfare

Cyberwarfare is primarily developed and used in military organizations, and the military sense of this term refers to various forms of military activity. These are as follows:

– classical, kinetic warfare, supported by modern IT;

– the use of information in a war zone;

– parallel warfare to create proper psychological conditions;

– asymmetric warfare[28] between countries in cyberspace.

Certain areas are becoming an important factor of victory or supremacy over the enemy or the opposite country, and this is why world superpowers devote significant resources to the development and upgrading of the existing warfare. In the United States, the debate on cyberwarfare was initiated by the Ministry of Defense in the early 1980s, and soon after, due to the need for military strategic adjustment to technological development, a new concept of warfare – C2W[29] – was developed, which contains the following elements: destruction, deception, psychological operations[30], operational security and electronic warfare [ARM 04]. After 1990, the United States began devoting a lot of attention to the development of network-centric warfare – NCW[31]. This

---

28 Asymmetric warfare is a term that explains the battle between belligerents whose relative military power, strategies or tactics differ significantly. It can also describe a conflict in which the resources for fighting differ significantly among the belligerents. Thus, each side uses its strengths and the weaknesses of the opponent to succeed.

29 Command and Control Warfare.

30 Psychological operations: countries' measures in the form of propaganda to influence the mental health of people and their decisions.

31 Network-Centric Warfare: transfer of information systems and technology in the military area by networking between well-informed geographically dispersed forces. The control system includes intelligence sensors, control and surveillance systems, and tools that enable accurate situational assessment and distribution of tasks [TOL 02]. The main idea is to integrate all combat systems over a computer network in order to command and control all units through that networked system.

has greatly increased the efficiency of military operations, and the way of fighting rose to a whole new level [WU 06]. NCW is a concept of information dominance/superiority, which allows greater military power, achievement of common awareness among decision makers and operatives, increased speed of command, faster implementation of operations, greater mortality and avoidance of unnecessary damage. It also implies the transfer of information knowledge to the military zone [ALB 06].

In 2002, the U.S. Department of Defense began with the establishment of GIG[32], as the spine of NCW, which was conceived on the basis of the system described previously. All the major systems involved in NCW are interconnected via GIG. Such a system will enable the collection, analysis, storage, sharing and management of confidential security information to be globally available to armed forces, legislators and support staff for the purposes of achieving information superiority [TOL 02]. It seems that information power and superiority became the fundamental targets of military superpowers. This confirms that ICT has revolutionary importance in achieving foreign policy interests, international security and world peace. Traditional forms of warfare are gradually declining and are increasingly complemented by modern technology and, in some cases, replaced by asymmetric-electronic warfare.

According to an American doctrine[33], electronic warfare involves the use of electromagnetic energy to control the electromagnetic environment or to carry out an attack on the opponent. It includes the following subcategories [ARM 04]:

– Electronic attack (the use of electromagnetic energy to attack personnel, facilities or equipment, in order to damage, neutralize or destroy the enemy's military capability).

---

32 Global Information Grid.
33 JP 3-51, Joint Doctrine for Electronic Warfare.

– Electronic protection (active and passive measures to protect personnel, facilities and equipment against electronic attacks by enemies or allies).

– Electronic combat support (activities under the command of the operational leader in order to search, intercept, identify and localize (un)intentional electromagnetic energy with a view to identify potential threats and plan operations).

IT also took care of the effective offensive and defensive operations of the army in the physical domain. One of the projects that falls within the scope of cyberwarfare is FCS[34], which places emphasis on advanced robotics, including autonomous unmanned vehicles. The aim is to create a combat system, which would be as interconnected as the Internet, as mobile as mobile phones and as intuitive as a video game. In addition to the development of new technologies, the United States is constantly updating its existing cyberunits, creating new hacker groups, carrying out information operations and limiting access points, which could be exploited for an attack. In doing so, the United States is not alone, since more than 120 countries have already developed or are developing this type of information attack [COL 08].

In recent years, more and more countries are aware of the benefits of cyberspace warfare, and have, thus, begun to develop their own capacities of cyber and asymmetric warfare. Since these are relatively new concepts, the traditional forms of kinetic war still remain in use. This is also because the consequences of cyberwar do not meet the effects of traditional warfare. However, the upgrading of warfare with ICT is resulting in greater efficiency, speed and accuracy of warfare. In the military field, cyberwarfare in the form of electronic warfare rarely appears as a single activity, since it is always combined with physical

---

34 Future Combat Systems, primarily developed between 2001 and 2009.

destruction. Berkowitz [BER 03] found that cyberwarfare, in the form of an attack on the opponent's information systems, makes sense only when it is part of a broader or larger plan. In his opinion, it should be used only if there are no better options available and when it is clear that such activity will help to win the war or provide a strong advantage over opponents. Strategic cyberwarfare is usually only used as a means of support, which refers to the use of ICT in the context of national and international security, in particular to determine the possible forms of the vulnerability of critical infrastructure in developed countries [SIR 06]. For providing support to the achievement of national and international interests, modern technology is also used in other areas, such as politics, diplomatic relations and control over the population. ICT is not only used as a means of support to military operations, but also as a tool for implementing information operations and propaganda activities, which are an integral part of modern cyberwarfare.

2.4.3. *Information operations*

Information operations have become an integral part of the national study of domestic and foreign environments and its influence on people's psychological state and their mentality. The level of development and use of such activities depends on the policies of individual countries and their interests in their own territory and beyond. Certainly, the global powers, such as the USA, China, Russia and others, have devoted a lot of attention to covert psychological activities, which are based on the use and misuse of information, very early, thus making information operations an integral part of the national cyberwarfare.

In 2003, under the auspices of the U.S. Department of Defense, a document, entitled *Information Operations Roadmap*, was adopted in the field of NCW. This document is a very good example of how the United States is trying to keep in step with the time of the increasing number of threats and exploiting new opportunities offered by innovation in IT. According to this document, the fundamental task of information operations is to dominate the electromagnetic environment by preventing, destroying and changing enemy threats, supervisory and control systems and critical infrastructure systems [TOL 02]. The target of information operations is a target group that the country wants to subdue; therefore, all activities are aimed at that target group to conduct or refrain from conducting a certain activity. In practice, such operations are most often used in counter-terrorism activities. In doing so, various tactics of deception, psychological operations and electronic warfare are used, which consequently form one's opinion and impact the society. Attacks on computer systems, negative publicity in the media, spam and threats with the failure of the infrastructure are the main symptoms of information operations [ARM 04]. By conducting information operations, perpetrators observe the interest (war) area, analyze the events and direct forces [JOY 01]. In addition, the instructions in the aforementioned document stipulate that appropriate psychological operations conducted through the media and the Internet require the constant monitoring of developments in the country of interest, even in times of peace [TOL 02].

Information operations are carried out in the form of strategic campaigns/operations throughout the whole spectrum of each conflict: from peace to war and vice versa. One of the latest areas of information operations, developed together with modern technology, is the computer network attack. According to the U.S. definition, an attack on a computer network covers disturbances, disabling, damage or destruction of information on computers and computer networks, or the destruction of computers and networks as such. In addition to electronic attacks via the Internet, this activity also includes physical attacks on computer systems and networks; however, it is rarely used in the military sector [ARM 04]. Information operations are rarely used in the social (non-war) sphere, but this does not mean that countries do not exploit the power of information to exert influence on their own populations. Activities, which are similar to information operations, take place daily within the national territory and are carried out by the authorities and politicians. In this case, ICT is misused for the purposes of propaganda activities, which is one example of the state influencing the minds of the people into condoning state actions. The developments in the United States after the terrorist attacks of September 11, 2001 are a great example of such activities.

2.4.4. *Propaganda activity*

By relying on software tools and information, cyberwarfare goes beyond combat in cyberspace; however, it also implies the abuse of information and the use of such information in a specific target area for directing human behavior. People are exposed to such an imposition of biased information on a daily basis, especially by politics and through the media. Such propaganda usually consists of the following activities [SCH 03]:

– Too much information by the media: providing enough information, which reduces the need to search for others.

– Ideological calls: calls to patriotism, protection of national interests.

– Discouraging information: what is really significant is of secondary importance in the media.

– Withholding information: selective disclosure of information.

– Cooperation and agreements: control over the media allows disinformation and an uncritical approach.

One of the best examples that demonstrates how misinformation and the closing of the information flow makes it possible to create a mental state, as pursued by the holder of the information power, is the flood of carefully selected information after September 11, 2001, when the United States experienced one of the most extensive terrorist attacks in history. After this attack, the U.S. government began an aggressive campaign on the war on terror in order to justify its own military actions in the Middle East. Despite the fact that the American public was outraged by the terrorist attack, it was necessary to encourage stronger emotions in people in order for the public to accept a (disproportionate and unjustified) military response. The government managed to achieve this by embarking on strong propaganda and psychological operations.

The provision of information about the terrorist attacks of September 11, 2001 to the public, which was achieved through the media and in conjunction with government departments, was carried out by repeating the same ideas and messages on TV and radio stations, newspapers and on the Internet on a daily basis. Computer networks transmitted messages, such as "War on America" and "America's New War" [RAN 06]. Thus, the war became the main topic of discussion, and the media and the film industry agreed to participate in it, because it brought life into their work, and, more significantly, earnings and success [SCH 03]. Most successful journalists strengthened their reputation by reporting on the war.

Hollywood and the U.S. military had always been interconnected, but after the terrorist attacks, their cooperation strengthened further due to a campaign entitled GWOT[35]. The Pentagon and Disney/ABC agreed to participate in the making of a 13-part reality TV series about

---

35 Global War on Terrorism [SCH 03].

the life of soldiers in the war against terrorism. The filming took place under the guidance of Jerry Bruckheimer and Bertram van Munster, the famous directors. They gained direct access to the troops in Afghanistan, while Disney financed the entire project entitled *Profiles From the Front Line*. Movies such as *Black Hawk Down* and *Pearl Harbor* were also a product of the cooperation between the U.S. Department of Defense and the media industry. The Department provided all the necessary resources in return for the final product, which supports national interests and policies and creates military-friendly propaganda and positive images of the United States in both domestic as well as in foreign environments. In achieving these objectives, the government also offered technical assistance and cooperation in writing the script, which had to be adapted to the requirements of the U.S. military and government. However, such integration and cooperation did not occur only in the media, but also in the entertainment industry. The main purpose of integrating the U.S. Department of Defense with the University of South Carolina, Disney, Paramount Studios and NBC Universal was to develop pervasive computer simulation and animation technology for both entertainment and military needs. In return, Hollywood obtained the best equipment to create special effects, while the video game industry created an entirely new concept of military games, which it used to develop new ideas. The result of such cooperation is reflected, for example, in the *America's Army* computer game, where players can experience the adrenaline surge of an actual war engagement, while the U.S. Army received a new tool to recruit soldiers [WIN 08]. Other cases involving similar activities have sparked speculations about conspiracy theories. In particular, the developments of September 11, 2001 and beyond encouraged some theoreticians (e.g. [SIN 11]) to discuss the theory, which speculates that the attacks were carried out in order to provide an excuse for military operations in the Middle East and the supremacy of the United States in the world.

The control of information by the U.S. government in the events related to the September 11, 2001 attacks can be summarized in the following three steps [SCH 03]:

– Elimination of criticism and skepticism with the assistance of the media, which did not allow room for criticism of domestic policy. At the same time, the U.S. government condemned ideological Taliban fundamentalism, and intolerance gradually spread in the domestic media.

– The U.S. government invites the media to collaborate. Thus, it limits the publication of certain information and excludes all journalists from the war zones. Nevertheless, the media did not show any more criticism or concerns; this was even true for those who used to loudly defend the freedom of the press and speech. The media was willing to do anything, even accept censorship, in order to be able to participate and attend the American way of war.

– After controlling the media, the government has turned its attention to the film studios. The media, government and movie production made a plan to reinforce the justification and impact of the American War. The purpose was to present the U.S. government agencies as positive actors.

After the situation became accepted as a war situation, it was time for a military response. In October 2001, the Enduring Freedom operation in Afghanistan, accompanied by the *War on Terrorism* and *America Strikes Back* slogans, took over global online networks. The declaration of War on Terror, as advertised, was determined prudently because nobody wanted terrorists to win. It was easy to accept the promise and predict actions, even though there was no consensus on what that really meant. After the 2001 attack, the then U.S. President G.W. Bush promised in his speech to "erase all evil in this world" as well as "chase villains and barbaric people". The use of straightforward terms [RAN 06], such as adversary or terrorist, did not last long, which is why these definitions were later supplemented by putting a face to the terms by identifying Osama bin Laden and Saddam Hussein. The described American propaganda activities represent a textbook example of taking an active role in the management of information, which was carried out with flying colors.

Politics, the media, film and gaming industries, thus, joined forces to exert psychological pressure on the American population in order to avoid their concerns and criticism regarding the situation in Iraq and Afghanistan. The terrorist attack was an excuse for the USA to invade the Middle East and take control of events and resources there. The American population, subjected to a unilateral, aggressive and very hostile campaign, succumbed to the psychological impact for a certain amount of time, which enabled the army to carry out their plan smoothly. However, this psychological impact only lasted for a short period of time.

As was demonstrated in this case, information in modern times cannot be controlled permanently. Although the U.S. media were under government control, the rest of the media in the world, especially in Europe, did not share the same views on the American war strategy. Skepticism and disapproval of the American ways quickly spread across Europe, and was also gradually transferred to the USA. Americans acquired the desired information from the online network of foreign countries [SCH 03]. This demonstrates that one can only possess the information power for a short period of time and that this component is extremely inconsistent and unpredictable. However, the American propaganda and campaign against terrorism were so successful that the government could bring the set military strategy to an end. This case also shows that cyberwarfare can provide very good support to classic warfare. In addition, the example of September 11, 2001 shows that cyberwarfare techniques are not actively used only by countries or governments, but also by civil groups, the media, NGOs, religious and ideological groups, and commercial entities.

Although it is difficult to discuss the independence of the media in modern times, since the cases described previously make it clear that the media is often under the influence of other interest groups, it is worth mentioning that the Internet is a place in which we can achieve the greatest possible independence. This is demonstrated by certain Websites that publish information about diplomatic talks and cables (e.g. [WIK 11]), and by the uncensored coverage of the events and arrangements, which informs the public about the activities of the main sources of information and decision making. The question arises whether these media groups are also influenced by other interest groups, since their operation and the collection of data require a great deal of funds.

On the basis of these examples of state cyberwarfare, it is possible to conclude that ICT can be used as an aid or a tool in state warfare. ICT is used as a tool when the performance of an attack takes place in the information environment. However, when technology is used in the physical world as an upgrade to existing warfare techniques, ICT can be considered as an aid for the performance of the attack, which can be more closely connected to espionage and not only to the production of modern/information weapons. This is why cyberwarfare techniques, as well as cyberespionage, are also used by organizations in the business sector to obtain confidential information on competitive opponents.

2.5. Organizations and cyberwarfare

During this period of capitalism and globalization, competition between commercial organizations has become very aggressive; often well beyond the permitted limits. Competition is forcing organizations to continuously develop and improve. Currently, larger organizations, mostly from the Western countries, have a greater advantage. Organizations lagging behind are using various methods in order to keep pace with the leaders. These methods are usually permitted and are based on proprietary or freely accessible information. There are certain organizations that are reaping benefits at the expense of other competitors. Unauthorized access to information and their abuse is a part of cyberwarfare, which belongs to the organizational or private sector.

In a review of research on cyberwarfare, which encompassed the period between 1990 and mid-2005, Knapp and Boulton [KNA 06] identify several important guidelines:

– a significant increase in cybercrime and cyberwarfare from one year to the next;

– less onerous barriers to unauthorized access;

– a large quantity and accessibility of tools to access information systems;

– high dependency on ICT organizations (private industry became the primary target);

– increasing use of ICT for industrial espionage;

– attacks on small businesses and individuals.

A comprehensive interpretation of these guidelines leads to the conclusion that cyberwarfare has overgrown the military framework and expanded into the commercial realm. The modern definitions of cyberwarfare gradually omit its military nature and increasingly explain this phenomenon as a manipulation of information to gain competitive advantage [WAL 07]. Today, commercial organizations dictate the guidelines for adapting to the information age and IT. Those who are able to make good use of information power and ICT in a competitive battle assume power and control in a competitive environment [ALB 06].

In contrast to previous experience, the trend of using and defining development guidelines is subordinated to the requirements of private industry. In the past, such development was dictated by the state, which was also the first to benefit from its advantages. In the information revolution period, the organizational environment provided guidelines for further development, which also influenced the field of cyberwarfare. To obtain a competitive edge, organizations exploited every possibility provided by ICT, which increased the opportunities for the abuse and destruction of competitive information.

The illegal obtention of information about other organizations falls within the scope of industrial espionage, which is part of intelligence activities. This method of secret data collection has been known for a long time. In the past, this kind of activity had a positive connotation, as it represented the spreading of ideas and progress; today, however, it represents a serious threat to the success and existence of large and developed companies. The executive branch of power used to have a monopoly over intelligence services; they represented an important source of a country's military and political power, and were a sign of its sovereignty. In the global world of the information age, the shift from geo-politics to geo-economics has meant that intelligence activities have also spread to the enterprise sector. Intelligence activities have, thus, become an important and fast-growing economic branch. This does not raise concerns if the organization's intelligence activities are conducted responsibly and if such activities are completely legal and ethical. Yet, some companies are using other methods, such as theft of information, wiretapping and searching offices, which means that they are surpassing the limit of what is allowed [POD 06].

Spying for foreign information is closely linked to another factor of organizational cyberwarfare, i.e. the spreading of falsehoods about the competitive organization or defamation.

This also involves cases related to the misuse of information or disinformation by people with a view to achieve a competitive edge. One such example was witnessed in 2011, when results of an alleged piece of research, which found that the average IQ of Microsoft Explorer users was lower than the IQ of those using other browsers, was published on the Internet. There is no better topic to ignite a war in both camps, which is why it is not surprising that this publication caused quite a stir. It was also cited in some eminent newspapers, such as the Telegraph, but it later turned out to be a prank [BBC 11]. This causes an enormous financial loss and the loss of reputation and trust of customers and partners for the competitors. In such cases, the perpetrators do not need to apply specific cybercrime techniques, and can easily achieve their goals. Apart from defamation, industrial espionage is also a common example of cyberwarfare at the organizational level.

2.5.1. *Industrial espionage*

Knowledge that enriches intellectual capital is the main factor for the successful operation of a certain organization. An organization can obtain such knowledge from its own work or from others. If knowledge cannot be obtained in such a way, it can also be acquired illegally by stealing from the competition, bribery, hacking intrusions to information systems, etc. The uncompromising struggle with the competition often requires one to walk on the very edge of what is possible and permissible. The information obtained in such a way often enables organizations to launch their product on the market before it would be presented by another company. Damage that occurs to the harmed organization can be irreparable [ROB 99]. Espionage is a form of intelligence activity that involves penetration to areas where confidential information is kept [SMI 10]. It is an activity carried out by spies on behalf of and for the purposes of foreign intelligence agencies and their countries.

If this occurs in the economic sphere, it is described as economic espionage [POD 08], which falls under economic intelligence. It is usually based on the collection of data from publicly available sources and is therefore lawful. Even reverse engineering, whereby a company considers its rival products, falls within the gray area. Specialized organizations, which collect information and inform their customers of any possible changes in the market against payment, also operate in this area [SCI 10].

Industrial espionage developed for the same reasons as intelligence activities, which are usually part of the state sector. The inaccessibility and confidentiality of the information has forced malicious people to steal and abuse it. The need for development and the competitiveness of the private sector has become the primary motivation of most organizations. Those who cannot or do not want to achieve this in a legitimate and legal way use a variety of techniques for unauthorized penetration.

It should be noted that the victims are not the targets of industrial espionage. They just represent the means of obtaining relevant information. The target of industrial espionage is data, and its form is irrelevant. The perpetrator attempts to obtain confidential or sensitive information that competitive organizations do not want to share with others. Damage caused as a result of industrial espionage is most commonly and most obviously manifested in material form. The damage assessment of such occurrences is difficult because organizations rarely report it. The recognition of damage may jeopardize the trust of customers and business partners, and may cause employees to lose their jobs. Organizations remain silent for the same reasons, which is why they do not disclose confidential information to the public[36]. Because of the severity of the consequences,

---

36 Numerous studies show that as many as 70–80% of illegal access cases are performed by company employees. An interesting fact is that companies report only 5–10% of such cases. Most often offenders are simply fired.

organizations protect their information assets, which competitors want to acquire by using sophisticated technology, security systems and laws, but in principle every item of information is accessible regardless of how protected it is. The only question is, "how much money and time is one willing to invest in the demolition of barriers?" [POD 08]. In doing so, organizations are very open to the available tips and techniques. Activities, skills and policy of the opponents are of paramount concern to them. In addition, this activity allows avoiding strategic surprises and ensures support for long-term decisions, gaining professional skills and providing protection and security of confidential information [LOW 06].

Industrial espionage takes place on several levels. It involves countries, international organizations and individuals [BER 74][37]. It can be part of a national intelligence activity or an individual organization. In the latter case, pharmaceutical, chemical and automobile industries are most vulnerable. Thefts of fashion collections and of the marketing plans of larger organizations also frequently occur. Such activities are constantly faced with threats, among which industrial espionage is one of the most serious, as it attacks their most important asset –

There are many reasons for taking such a decision, but above all companies assess whether the public recognition of such an attack would have a negative impact on their reputation and business [GAO 07]. The public recognition of the organization's security system breakthrough would lead to a lack of confidence in the organization at all levels, which would be reflected on the stock market as well as in customers' behavior, which could be diverted to (apparently) safer competitors. In addition, existing customers or investors could require the recovery of any damages incurred. The organization is even more vulnerable in the period following the attack. Public recognition would also mean the recognition of weaknesses in information system security, which would attract further attacks. Another reason for the concealment of such attacks is undoubtedly a lack of confidence that organizations and the general public have in law enforcement agencies responsible for the detection of cybercrime perpetrators [RIC 07].

37 Bergier is a pioneer in the field of industrial espionage [BER 74].

knowledge. Attacks on commercial systems are extremely sophisticated, and there are more and more people who are willing to perform them. China employs a million agents in this field, which enables it to seriously harm the global infrastructure. Russia is also among the most powerful countries, which increasingly uses the possibilities offered by the Internet to retrieve vital information to solve its economic development[38] despite a smaller number of agents in comparison to China [CON 09]. Methods of industrial spies using the latest developments in ICT and other technologies have become so dangerous that many fear this will lead to the end of any kind of private life and to the disintegration of our society. However, the future, at least in this field, is difficult to predict due to constant changes. Today, certain methods are valid, but tomorrow they might not be anymore. Procedures that have proven to be effective in one country could, if they were used in another country, end with painful setbacks. Nevertheless, there are classical methods[39], which are used individually or in combination by almost all spies to obtain information about the competition.

---

38 Sectors that are most exposed to industrial espionage include the automotive industry, industrial sectors related to renewable energy sources, communications, optics, X-ray technology, machinery and research.

39 Such methods include the study of competition's publications and summaries of lawsuits; the data provided by openly telling former employees of the competition; market research and reports of boards of engineers; financial reports; fairs, exhibitions, and brochures of the competition; the analysis of competing products; reports of salesmen and purchasing departments; attempts to hire technicians employed by the competition and fulfilling questionnaires; tactful questions for technicians employed by the competition during technical congresses; direct covert observations; false job offers for employees of the competition without attempting to employ them, but instead obtaining information from them; false negotiations with competitors under the pretext that one wants to acquire a license for one of their patents; the recruitment of professional spies to obtain information; soliciting competition staff to leave their jobs in order to obtain information from them; the abuse/damage of competitor's property; bribery of purchasing departments or employees of the competition; the infiltration of agents among employees or technicians of the competition; illegal wiretapping, theft of samples and documents; extortion and various means of coercion [BER 74].

Espionage seldom uses violent methods, since the objective is to obtain information secretly. The aim of the spy is, thus, to gain access to the information and pass it to the desired location without being noticed [ELL 10]. Today, these goals can be achieved in a much easier way. In the digital age, the Internet, which connects the world in a large global network, is certainly an inevitable means or method to achieve these objectives. The information has, thus, become accessible at a distance, whereas traces of an unauthorized entry or access to them are often not observed or detected. It seems that industrial espionage guidelines will not change. Aggressive competition and companies lagging behind will demand ever new guidelines and needs for industrial espionage. New emerging technical equipment for intelligence services, which is also available to spies, enables the fulfillment of such needs. The fight for information in the organizational sphere, which we may use to retain or guarantee business success, has become extremely sophisticated and subtle in the information age, and therefore gives an impression that it does not even exist. The public does not expose it, the law enforcement authorities rarely deal with it, while organizations are using it more and more frequently. The disclosure of business secrets to reduce the opponent's reputation, the theft of information to achieve the advantages, negative media propaganda and the denigration of competition are just some of the most common forms of cyberwarfare in the business world of the modern information society.

There are also cases of state capture. This phenomenon describes a case where a certain country and its property are held hostage by various (criminal, mafia) networks who aim to avoid state laws, policies and regulations for (mostly financial) benefits with the assistance of corrupt public officials and politicians. In this case, the role of ICT is to control transactions, while the misuse of data in cyberspace helps to carry out the supervision of and the provision of guidance to corrupt people.

2.5.2. *Politically and ideologically motivated groups – perpetrators of cyberwarfare*

In addition to countries and organizations, civil entities are also aware of the advantages of the use and misuse of ICT. Thus, they represent the third group of offenders or actors in cyberwarfare. Civil actors primarily include politically motivated groups, which use cyberspace in order to achieve desired goals. Political motivation most often includes cyberterrorism, but this is not an isolated case. Apart from terrorists, this group also includes activists and protesters who often attend organized political events in cyberspace. Political motivation is not the only reason for which civic groups abuse the information power and use it for fighting against those who have other opinions. These also include other interest groups that are not necessarily politically motivated and that attack counter or hostile groups very aggressively by applying the techniques of cyberwarfare. Anderson [AND 08] states that there has been a significant increase in the misuse of ICT for the destruction of existing political, social and commercial structures in recent years. In this field, Anderson classifies activities aimed at espionage, antiglobalization, international conflicts, anarchism, workers' revolts, environmental movements and the fight for animal rights. Information is often misused to support national interests, where hacktivists or adherents of ECD[40] are the most aggressive. These include movements related to antiglobalization, animal rights, workers' rights, the fight against genetically modified food, wars, environmental change, piracy organizations, etc. Just like countries or organizations, various interest clubs also resort to techniques of cyberwarfare; however, they do so for other reasons. The basic motive of these political and other interest groups is to obtain the necessary information and to pass it to as many people as possible by means of ICT.

---

40 Electronic Civil Disobedience.

Informing the public of what is happening "behind the scenes" can actually contribute to the demolition of the elites who control the economy or to the preservation of such elites in their acquired positions through the management of information. Drawing attention to the pressing issues in which they are engaged is their primary objective. This also facilitates the detection of a variety of problems in the international community, such as international terrorism, and, indirectly, enables control of the country in terms of its independent organizations and individuals. Such cases of control are characterized by a hidden trap, since certain seemingly independent organizations and individuals can point to particular problems and (re)direct the public's attention to them, while at the same time ensuring that the elite continues to maintain its position, which in turn provides for the protection of such elites.

During the 2011 riots and protests in the United Kingdom, the British government considered banning social networks precisely because ICT was used as a support tool for the protest movements; they also worked with manufacturers of consumer technologies in order to investigate and pursue these riots and protests. Arguments related to the fact that the riots were better organized because of social networking sites, and were thus much more severe, prolonged and violent, often appeared in the media. The use of ICT for political purposes, such as the organization of protests and revolts, is becoming more common, as the Internet is a good means of communication, coordination and planning of actions. Cyberwarfare in such cases does not cover illegal techniques, but only uses modern technology to successfully carry out actions in the physical environment. Cybercrime techniques aimed at achieving political objectives have been used, for example, in the 2010 cyberattack on Myanmar. This attack prevented normal access to the Internet throughout the country. The target of the DDOS[41] attack was the Ministry of Postal and Telecommunication Services, which acts as the main hub of the country's Internet infrastructure. The Myanmar elections were the reason for the attack, since censorship there is still very strict [MYA 10].

To achieve certain goals set by cyberwarriors, cyberwarfare was also used in August 2011, when the AntiSec hacker group published a 10 GB file containing confidential documents belonging to the police and the FBI on the Internet. These documents included personal information, e-mail addresses, passwords, data about denunciators, social security numbers, data of stolen credit cards, etc. By publishing such data, the hacking group also acquired some money which they later donated to various support groups [MIL 11]. A month earlier, the same hacking group broke into Apple's servers and stole information about the user accounts of some of the most important users – administrators [O'GR 11]. In the same month, this group, in collaboration with Anonymous, a political hacktivist group, broke into a database of the Man Tech Company, which has concluded a 5-year contract with the FBI to provide Internet security for the U.S. government [RAS 11].

Other civilian groups, similar to politically motivated groups, are also extremely agressive actors in cyberwarfare, using the same techniques but with different motives. To draw attention to their own ideological goals, beliefs, actions and recruiters, they exploit ICT and, in some cases, also implement systems intrusions, thefts of information and similar actions.

The pattern characterizing the functioning of civil society organizations is similar, whereas there is most often no attempt to destroy or damage information (with the exception of cyberterrorists), but to disclose such

41 Distributed Denial of Service – massive attack on a specific service with the assistance of infected computers – zombies.

information to the greatest possible number of people. Cyberspace is a very good tool to spread ideas and point to the problems associated with their activities. To obtain information, such groups often employ illegal techniques, especially intrusions into information systems, and online fraud techniques for gaining access to them. Just like terrorists in cyberspace, other interest groups combine the advantages of the cyber environment with traditional activities in the real world in order to maximize their impact. Cyberattacks are not the primary goal, but ICT is used to support (planning, communication, etc.) activities in the physical world.

Information, which may constitute a compromise of individual entities, is not published only by the politically and ideologically motivated groups. The publication of information by the state also enables citizens to obtain an insight into the events carried out by government departments and thus gain appropriate control. An Internet-based service of the Slovenian Commission for the Prevention of Corruption entitled *Supervizor*, which "enables the general public, the media, professionals, and government agencies to gain an insight into the expenditure of public institutions, which refer to goods and services" [SUP 11], represents a good example of such publication. The public exposure of financial flows between the public and private sectors increases the responsibilities of public office holders for the effective and efficient use of public funds, provides a reasoned discussion of measures taken and investments planned, and reduces the risk of mismanagement, abuse of authority and, in particular, limits the systemic corruption, unfair competition and clientelism. In this case, the political motivation goes in the opposite direction – the state provides information to the public, which exercises control over its operation and reduces the interdependence between politics and the management of the country.

2.6. The role of countries in cyberwarfare

Politically motivated cybercrime evolved in the 1980s and will, according to Anderson [AND 08], keep on gaining importance, becoming more dangerous and expansive. The use of the Internet for communication, coordination and the establishment of public relations will dramatically increase. Anderson believes that online protests will increase, while users will at the same time combine activities in the real world. A flood of information in modern times will require more aggressive and more widespread campaigns or attacks from these groups, in order for them to attract media attention, which is their primary goal.

Cyberwarfare does not merely involve some countries as perpetrators and some as victims. Cyberwarfare is involved in all social spheres, it is all around us, and we encounter it every day. Every individual has used a fighting technique to gain information at least once in their lives, but this was not necessarily illegal and was mostly of no significance. In the context of cyberwarfare at the national level, among organizations, or by ideological, media and major interest groups, the warfare techniques and their consequences are often socially harmful. The struggle for information includes all countries and their entities. However, some are more aggressive than others, because they devote more resources to the development of this field.

Different countries, in terms of their size, economic performance and political orientation, understand the importance and benefits of cyberwarfare and develop its techniques. In fact, it is not clear which entities are more successful in achieving this. The involvement of ICT in government and organizational structures is not necessarily an advantage, since it can also represent a weakness in terms of risk. Countries mentioned as the main cyberwarriors (the United States, China and Russia) can be gradually equated with countries that are less dependent on

ICT, closed and inaccessible (e.g. North Korea). The United States is certainly the world's leading political, economic and military superpower, which makes it the most popular target for malicious intrusions and attacks on information systems. We could say that the U.S. government and economic authorities had no choice in their attempts to compete and counter this kind of challenge but to develop such a strong offensive and defensive cyberwarfare system.

2.6.1. *The United States*

In the United States, cyberwarfare is represented by the U.S. military strategy of proactive cyberdefense, while the use of cyberwarfare represents a platform for attack. "The Pentagon, trying to create a formal strategy to deter cyberattacks on the U.S., plans to issue a new strategy soon declaring that a computer attack from a foreign nation can be considered an act of war that may result in a military response" [SAN 11]. In the field of IT, the United States is not only the most advanced country in the world, but also the country most dependent on communication infrastructure. Therefore, it is the most vulnerable country from the perspective of the use of ICT. Because of such a situation, the United States implements various programs and activities in order to reduce vulnerability, particularly in the area of cyberwarfare, which received considerable attention in the past 20 years. They believe that, for example, in order to win the war, we first need to win the information war. All U.S. military successes in the past are attributed to its ability to achieve an information advantage over the enemy. On the other hand, any failure of the U.S. Army is attributed to their inability to achieve such an information advantage [BER 03]. The United States became the pioneer in setting up cybersecurity in 1988, when the first CERT[42] was established at the Carnegie Mellon University as a response to the increase in network attacks.

---

42 Computer Emergency Response Team.

Today, the U.S. CERT is part of the U.S. Department of Homeland Security and coordinates defensive measures and responses to attacks all over the country [HUG 09].

The creation of the Information Warfare Executive Board in 1995 was the most important step in achieving the goal of reduced vulnerability. Later, the most important directive in this area was adopted, i.e. PDD39[43], which governs policy in the field of terrorist threats and includes activities related to information warfare. A policy concerning critical infrastructure protection was adopted in 1998 on the basis of the PDD63 document, which sets up two specialized units: the National Infrastructure Protection Centre (NIPC) under the auspices of the FBI, and the Critical Infrastructure Assurance Office (CIAO) [SIR 06]. The main tasks of the CIAO include border and transport security, crisis response, chemical, biological, radiological and nuclear protection, information analysis and infrastructure protection.

In 1998, the United States in its National Program for Critical Infrastructure Protection (CIP) mentioned the need for cooperation between the private and state sectors at the national and international level. This led to the establishment of the NIPC in 1998, whose mission is to collect information on threats to infrastructure and point to potential attacks, state analysis, criminal investigation and response [JOY 01]. In addition, the National Infrastructure Assurance Council (NIAC) was established in 1999, followed by the National Plan for Information Systems Protection a year later [SIR 06]. In 2002, the U.S. government created the Department of Homeland Security, which later established eight new divisions, among others including the Commerce's Information Infrastructure Protection Institute. In addition to the CIAO, the U.S. Department of Commerce also manages the NIST[44] and NTIA[45]. The purpose of the NIST is

---

43 Presidential Decision Directive 39.
44 National Institute of Standards and Technology.
45 National Telecommunications and Information Administration.

to promote and raise global economic growth through cooperation with private organizations in the development and integration of technology, measures and standards[46] [ARM 04].

The United States did not only aim to provide the security of its own IT, and systems related to it at the political and legislative level, but also combined these efforts with the activities carried out by specific specialized military units, which had the fundamental task to defend the United States' critical and military infrastructure. Many American units and all of their major military agencies (the army, navy and air force) have developed the C2W concept and already began to train their members in C2W cells at the beginning of the 1990s. The legal acts narrowly defined the concept of C2W as cyberwarfare, but planning a strategy for the implementation of information operations in other countries was a very risky move, which is why it was kept strictly confidential until the end of the 20th Century. In 1995, the Uniformed Services of the United States established three new agencies in this field: the AFIWC[47], LIWA[48] and FIWC[49]. Since 2010, there are military units in the U.S. cyberspace and physical space, designed to protect and analyze the U.S. space and simultaneously threaten the opponent's cyberspace and physical space. These units, which have an impact on IT and organizations that are dependent on and intertwined with IT, include:

---

46 The basic tasks of the NIST [ARM 04] are as follows: providing assistance to industry in the development of technology and the increase of quality; modernization of production processes; ensuring product reliability; commercialization of developmental products; developing information security guidelines, procedures and technical solutions for the effective implementation of Office of Management and Budget (OMB) policies in government offices.

47 Air Force Information Warfare Centre.

48 Land Information Warfare Activity.

49 Fleet Information Warfare Centre.

– USCYBERCOM[50]: solely responsible for the defense of military computer networks and the performance of cyberattacks on military targets of hostile countries;

– ARCYBER[51]: intended for planning, coordination, networking operations and defense of all networks of the armed forces for cyberwarfare;

– US Marine Corps Forces Cyberspace Command: marine unit responsible for the protection of critical infrastructure against cyberattacks, including a unit of cryptologists;

– CYBERFOR[52]: unit designed to command and provide forces and equipment for cryptology, signal analysis and electronic warfare;

– 24 AF[53]: unit of the Air Force, whose purpose is cyberwarfare [BRA 11];

– Cyber Command (CC): is part of the U.S. Strategic Command (USSTRATCOM). It was created as a response to increasingly aggressive digital threats of external origin (by foreign criminal groups, terrorist groups and individual hackers) that on a daily basis threatened the U.S. information and communications networks. The task of the CC is to manage the operations and defend specific activities within the Ministry of Defense, to plan integrated cyber operations, provide free activities and operations in cyberspace and prevent opponents from achieving the same things [ALE 11].

The U.S. Army also conducts training courses for cyberwarfare in the framework of the Space and Naval Warfare Systems Center. The purpose of the course is to teach participants how to properly respond to cyberattacks, especially in terms of intrusion detection, adequate protection of the networks and response to network attacks

---

50 United States Cyber Command.
51 Army Cyber Command.
52 Navy Cyber Forces.
53 24 Air Force.

[ALE 11]. In addition, the U.S. Army developed cyber weapons that can be used to disable an opponent's use of computer systems to attack the United States. These weapons include viruses that can damage the opponent's critical network infrastructure, in a way similar to what was done with Stuxnet[54]. In times of peace, the U.S. President has to approve the use of these types of "weapons" [NAK 11].

The FBI plays an important role in the prevention and prosecution of cyberattacks. If the source of attack is external, the investigation would include the CIA, and if the cyberattack also includes a financial attack, the USSS[55] becomes the main investigative agency. The U.S. Department of Defense and the National Security Agency (NSA) also have their own cybersecurity specialists [HUG 09].

In June 2011, the U.S. Department of Defense publicly announced, for the first time, that internet attacks on the United States, computer infrastructure sabotage and other cyber threats constitute an act of war, as stated at the beginning of this section. When performing such attacks, countries can thus expect a military response, even by involving traditional armed forces. This is an extract of the first Internet security strategy. It explicitly states that network attacks on critical infrastructure (military systems, railways, power plants, gas pipelines, oil pipelines, etc.) constitute an act of war. The Pentagon, thus, wants to deter attackers, who previously speculated that the United States will not respond to such attacks [GOR 11]. Obviously, the United States is well aware of the risks and benefits of cyberattacks, in which it is involved on a daily basis.

---

54 Stuxnet is a computer worm discovered in June 2010 that is believed to have been created by the United States and Israel to attack Iran's nuclear facilities.
55 United States Secret Service.

Because of the high dependence of the critical infrastructure on ICT, the establishment of national policies, plans and specialized units for the protection and detection of threats at this level was not only necessary but above all a wise decision. Statements made by Coleman [COL 08] confirm that, apart from the United States, techniques and tools for the purposes of cyberwarfare are being developed in approximately 120 countries, while we must also include terrorist and organized crime groups, which exacerbate the threats and risks even further.

Apart from the United States, some European countries, such as Germany, the Netherlands, Norway, Sweden, Switzerland, the United Kingdom, Austria, Finland, France and Italy, have also begun to implement vulnerability analyses of their national early warning infrastructures and to adopt legal acts in this area. The authors expect that sooner or later other European countries will also join them. By all means, cyberwarfare is not only used in the "Western world", but is also used increasingly profoundly and often very successfully in the countries from the "rest of the world".

2.6.2. *China*

Apart from the United States, the most powerful country in the field of cyberwarfare is China, since cyberwarfare is of critical and vital importance to the country. Despite the fact that China has the most populous traditional army[56], this does not give it an advantage over the highly technologically developed armies, such as the U.S. army, and any other enemy that is financially and technologically better equipped.

---

56 China's military consists of 2.3 million soldiers. In comparison, the USA has the second largest army, i.e. 1.38 million soldiers, followed by India with 1.3 million members of the armed forces and Russia with 1.24 million soldiers [BEZ 09].

China invests its available resources in asymmetric forms of warfare in an attempt to catch up in development and stand side by side with the world's military superpowers. China's research into the nature of cyberwarfare originates from two primary sources: foreign countries, especially the United States, and a combination of ancient Chinese philosophy and military experience. For the purposes of theoretical research and the development of this field, China integrated traditional military[57] philosophy, since it had neither the possibility or the ability to fully implement the American theory and practice. The Chinese cyberwarfare theory thus covers the following [WU 06]:

– Defensive cyberwarfare – non-technical methods, such as concealment, camouflage and disinformation that can overcome the technological gap[58].

– Offensive cyberwarfare – the weaker force can defeat the stronger force in case of an early or unexpected attack. At the moment, China is only capable of cyberattacks and does not have the ability to develop and implement NCW[59], while the United States has developed this concept of fighting down to the last detail.

Cyberwarfare is further divided into the following subcategories [WU 06]:

– NCW – physical warfare supported by ICT.

– Electronic war to control the electromagnetic environment.

– Network war over computer networks for access to military systems.

– Psychological operations using media deception and propaganda.

---

57 Sun Tzu: The Art of War, Mao Zedong: People's War, 36 Strategies.
58 This idea has proved to be futile in the case of the American Desert Storm operation, in which Iraqi troops were unable to escape or hide from satellite-guided missiles.
59 Network-Centric Warfare.

Chinese cyberwarfare tactics include assault and destruction of the electromagnetic environment, attacks on computer networks, deception, control, manipulation of information and disinformation, encryption and decryption, and psychological diverting of attention. Techniques and methods of this type of cyberwarfare coincide with China's objectives of overcoming the skills, power and technology of other countries with military power. Through the acquisition of foreign military knowledge, China will quickly catch up with the world's greatest powers, which will allow it to compete, while an independent development of their own technology would take too much time, human and financial resources [FRI 08].

Just like the United States, China also invested in the implementation of cyberwarfare in practice and through its integration into political, economic, research and military spheres, in addition to the theoretical and scientific development of this concept. According to the available data, Chinese institutions engaged in developing and understanding cyberwarfare include the following [WU 06]:

– Military Strategy Research Centre – PLA[60] Institute of Science, which is the largest research center for cyberwarfare in China (its purpose is to develop a strategic military theory of cyberwarfare, integrate it into all military operations, develop and organize tactics, and participate in the international ICT community);

– PLA Institute of Electronic Technology, which engages in the study and development of new technologies in order to focus on the technical aspects of cyberwarfare development;

– PLA Joint Staff-3;

– National Intelligence Property and Computer System Research Centre;

---

60 People's Liberation Army.

– Cheng-Do University of Electronic Science and Technology;

– Shanghai Technology and Physics Department;

– China Institute of Science.

According to estimates of the U.S. Department of Defense, the Chinese Army (PLA) is supposed to be developing computer viruses and techniques for penetrating the foreign computer systems of their opponents [USS 99] and has also created a simulation center for cyberwarfare. Chinese military strategy includes the knowledge regarding methods used to create and plant a computer virus, perform intrusions into information systems of other countries and implement ICT-based psychological warfare [RAW 05]. China has set up its own battalions in cyberspace and adopted legal arrangements aimed at identifying and exploiting the vulnerabilities of foreign armed forces, governments and commercial sectors. China officially recognized that it equates cyberspace with air, land and sea, and developed a special military branch for this purpose [ALE 11]. In addition, the U.S. military identified a total of five Chinese cyberwarfare bases where the Chinese authorities are supposed to be recruiting professionals and other people talented in the field of technology, and also training their own troops for this purpose. Thus, China greatly increased the knowledge, capacity and capability of military forces, which should be fully capable of taking over the position of a world superpower and of successfully implementing international military operations [WU 06].

China has also officially confirmed that it has set up an elite group of warriors in the Internet space. It is called the Blue Army[61] and consists of about 30 skilled hackers who form a team and were chosen from among the best. Some come from the PLA, others are officers, students and other members of society. Officially, the mission of the Blue Army

---

61 Blue Army: China CyberWarriors [SIA 12].

is to protect China against external Internet attacks, but they should not initiate attacks themselves. The Chinese newspaper *PLA Daily* reported that simulated cyberattacks on China were carried out with the aim of training the Blue Army. The attackers were four times more numerous than the Blue Army and tried to overwhelm the Chinese network with viruses, worms, spam, and to infiltrate it, but the Blue Army convincingly won. The recognition of the existence of such units is no surprise, since security experts have long observed that the largest share of cyberattacks is coming from China [LEW 11].

Despite intensive efforts and scientific research, China still lags behind the military capacity of Western countries. The concept of cyberwarfare has become the lifeline that places Asia, and especially China, on the list of largest potential attackers in terms of cyberwarfare. China represents a threat in terms of the use of ICT and its exponential implementation in Chinese society, and (so far?) not in terms of knowledge.

Although the Internet enables people around the world to access to huge amounts of information, the situation in China is different. At the request of the Chinese government, companies such as Microsoft, Google and Yahoo arranged their technology for the Chinese market and thus changed the Internet into a cyber tool of state repression. The example of China shows that control of the Internet and ICT is possible, although not entirely. In this respect, China was also followed by other countries around the world, such as Yemen, Vietnam, Malaysia, Burma, Tunisia, Egypt and to some extent Singapore [WIN 08].

2.6.3. *Russia*

After the collapse of the Soviet Union, Russia, similarly to China, saw an opportunity to use cyberwarfare to develop asymmetric warfare and overcome the gap in the traditional military field. According to publicly available information, which is quite scarce, Russia has four institutions primarily responsible for information security [THO 98]:

– Security Council, responsible for the protection of national interests, which may be the target of cyberwarfare;

– Federal Agency for Government Communications and Information (FAPSI), whose task is to protect government communications systems;

– State Technical Commission, an agency dedicated to the development of international law, licensing and certification of information warfare-related policies;

– Russian Armed Forces, responsible for the analysis of cyberwarfare impacts on the Russian army.

Although Russia's activities in cyberwarfare are difficult to detect due to their confinement and confidentiality, it is possible to connect Russia with cyberattacks on Estonia in 2007, Georgia, Azerbaijan and South Ossetia in 2008, and Poland in 2009 [SHA 10, TOD 08, CIV 08].

A very good and understandable example of an information cyberattack occurred in April 2007 when Estonia became the victim of such an attack. It only took a few minutes for the websites of leading Estonian banks and media to cave in. Even the government communication system was compromised [DAV 07]. The attacked networks included Websites of the Estonian president, the major news agencies, ministries and the two largest Estonian banks [TRA 07]. Attempts to identify the perpetrators showed that at least one of the attacks came from a Russian state institution, while the rest of these attacks came from all over the world, so this hypothesis could not be proved [JUR 08]. A few days after the cyberattack on Estonia, the country witnessed general panic and unrest, which left more than 150 people injured and one Russian citizen dead (Estonia Hit by "Moscow CyberWar"; [BBC 07]). A similar event occurred in 2008, just before Russia's army attacked Georgia, when information systems of the Georgian military defense unit failed [KRE 08]. A few weeks before the actual military attack on Georgia, the country also experienced a cyberattack. Security experts noticed several DOS attacks on Georgian servers, followed by the disfigurement of Websites. Shortly after the military attack, an attack on the communications of Georgian media and transportation companies also occurred. Despite the fact that Russia denied being responsible for the attacks, the USA security experts claim they have clear evidence that the attacks were carried out by the Russian Business Network, a Russian criminal hacking group. Allegedly, there is evidence that the Georgian Internet traffic is routed through Russia's (especially Moscow's) telecommunications companies, which gives Russian authorities the ability to control the Georgian internet [MAR 08].

It is clear that cyber operations are possible, feasible and present in warfare. The example of the cyberattack on Estonia shows that no country is safe from this kind of threat and that the widespread implementation of ICT in all spheres of society, and especially in different authorities, is not always the best idea. Even Slovenia, which is, by experts, often compared to Estonia due to its development and history (e.g. [WSB 05]), is undoubtedly under threat in terms of cyberwarfare, and in particular in terms of industrial and government espionage. An attempt to develop e-Slovenia along the lines of e-Estonia, therefore, might not be the most suitable or deliberate decision.

2.6.4. India[62]

In the field of software development, India is an extremely powerful country, but we know little about its activities in

---

62 Taken from Dalal [DAL 11], Tiwary [TIW 11] and Kaushik and Fitter [KAU 13].

cyberwarfare. After the cyberattack India experienced in the summer of 2012, in which officials from the Ministry of External Affairs, the Ministry of Home Affairs, the Defence Research and Development Organisation (DRDO) and the Indo-Tibetan Border Police (ITBP) were attacked and a lot of sensitive information was under threat, it was found that approximately 12,000 computers were affected. At that time, the responsibility for preventing attacks was assigned to the Indian Computer Emergency Response Team (CERT-In), which is a branch of the Department of Information Technology. CERT-In announced that the number of "cybersecurity breaches has grown from 23 in 2004 to 13,301 in 2011". Because of these breaches, the government divided the CERT-In, in order to better prepare the country for serious threats: "CERT-In now protects cyber assets in non-critical areas while a new body called the National Critical Information Infrastructure Protection Centre (NCIIPC) protects assets in sensitive sectors such as energy, transport, banking, telecom, defense, and space".

The government notes that more attention must be invested in research and development, whereas NCIIPC is preparing the final version of the national cybersecurity policy. In general, India has not suffered any major economic or physical harm due to cyberattacks. However, the government-owned Nuclear Power Corporation of India is at constant risk of security breach, since it continuously detects attacks, but is, in its opinion, able to successfully block them. India admits that its cyberwarfare defense strategy was tackled too late and, consequently, it detects attacks on their infrastructure, but is now increasingly preparing adequate strategies and focusing its expertise on the development of this field, so that in the future India will be able to defend itself from attacks and join other countries that are active in the field of cyberwarfare.

2.6.5. *Iran*

In terms of cyberwarfare, Iran is an interesting country due to the attack using the Stuxnet worm in 2010, which destroyed a large number of nuclear centrifuges for uranium enrichment. As already mentioned in one of the previous sections, the Stuxnet was a product of the US–Israeli intelligence services, which focused primarily on attacking and disabling the uranium enrichment capabilities in Iran. This is why the Islamic Republic of Iran decided to start building a cyberdefense and to actively engage in warfare, as demonstrated by the attacks on the United States, Israel, Saudi Arabia and the United Arab Emirates. Iran demonstrated its cyber capabilities to the rest of the world in the context of "naval exercises in the strategic Strait of Hormuz, the only way in and out of the Persian Gulf and a vital oil supply route", calling it cyberwarfare operations [UPI 13]. In particular, the aforementioned countries, such as the USA and Israel, wish to use their cyber operations to weaken Iran [CHU 13]. However, there is considerable doubt that Iran will keep on enduring these attacks, which is why a retaliatory blow could soon be expected. Iran's ability has been demonstrated by the above-mentioned attacks and by the recent attacks on Israel [KRA 13].

2.6.6. *Israel*

"The Israel Defense Forces has defined cyberwarfare as the fifth realm of warfare, alongside land, sea, air and space. The IDF has established a command dedicated to cyberwarfare that brings together personnel from the Intelligence Branch and the Teleprocessing Branch to ward off cyberattacks" [COH 13a]. This statement demonstrates that the existing active role in international cyberattacks in Israel was also formally supported by the army. Israel has already been very active in attacks mainly on Iran, and now its active presence in this domain is also formally endorsed. In addition to the cyberwarfare activities against Iran, especially together with the U.S. forces [CHU 13], Israel is extremely active in attacks on Palestinian targets [ABU 13]. Despite its small size, Israel has a high military capability and, as a strong ally of the United States, plays an active role in the Middle East, which is of great interest to the Western world due to its rich oil deposits. Although Israel defines its program of cyberwarfare as a distinctly defensive activity [COH 13a], the examples of attacks show that its orientation is quite the opposite, which has also been clearly confirmed by specialists. This is demonstrated by the examples related to the development of malicious software, e.g. Stuxnet, Duqu and Flame, which have been proven to (also) originate from Israel. Such software attacks Iran's information systems related to the development of nuclear facilities in the country.

2.6.7. *North Korea*

A high level of competence in the use of cyberwarfare technology and its implementation in all sectors of society is not the key to success. Bratusa [BRA 11] believes that a lack of dependence on IT is crucial for achieving an advantage. Bratusa [BRA 11] states that North Korea, which has developed average offensive skills, while it is characterized by a very low dependence on technology and well-designed defense, which includes filtering the entire Internet traffic and the possibility of selective Internet connection shutdown, which prevents countries from responding to its attack, is currently the most powerful country in the field of cyberwarfare.

Today, cyberwarfare is occurring in virtually all spheres of social life, and it represents a major challenge for many countries, as has already been argued. Many countries are intensively engaged in creating systems for protection and/or attacks. However, these are not presented here simply because they successfully hide their activities. Countries which are not (yet) seriously dealing with these issues will need to begin to develop a strategy for countering, defending and responding to attacks, without the current drawbacks of ICT, as soon as possible. Effective defense includes the ability to resist the flood of modern technology and balance its benefits and drawbacks. The disadvantage of a broad and comprehensive implementation of ICT was also observed in the case of cyberwarfare between Russia and Estonia. Despite its lower level of development in cyberwarfare, Russia skillfully took advantage of its ICT skills to support the interests of foreign policy and international relations. The main problem with interstate attacks, i.e. the international condemnation and joint actions against the attackers, is almost impossible to solve, since the legislation in the field of cyberwarfare adopted by the international community is inadequate and insufficient.

2.7. Efforts against cyberwarfare: international and national legislation

Because of its expansion, diverse forms, numerous actors, techniques and consequences, cyberwarfare represents a highly specific problem that challenges the existing international and national laws – the current situation is largely insufficient and ineffective. The legislation does not anticipate and does not relate to the integrity of cyberwarfare as a political, corporate or ideologically motivated cybercrime, but manages this field only partially and places it among the traditional and completely inflexible legal norms. International legal instruments and norms that are at least partly related to these issues include the international law of war, the Charter of the United Nations, the Geneva Convention, the Convention on Cybercrime, the international human rights law and certain international treaties and agreements, such as the North Atlantic Treaty Organization (NATO), which govern international cooperation in the prosecution and treatment of offenses, including cybercrime and cyberwarfare.

The legal regulation of cyberspace and activities therein, as well as the legal restrictions related to the detection, investigation and corroboration of unwanted activities, are the most important bases for an effective defense against malicious attacks by cyberwarriors. Without an adequate normative basis, the competent authorities cannot fight against this type of threat. The current state of legislation demonstrates that cyberwarfare is not awarded sufficient attention. The fundamental dilemma that represents the basis of the problems mentioned hereinafter is related to the identification and definition of cyberwarfare. Currently, there is no universal definition or consensus on what cyberwarfare is supposed to include, in what forms it is supposed to be carried out, and with which motives it could be identified. In addition, despite the established use of the term "cyberwar" and "cyberwarfare", we do not even know whether the words "war" and "warfare" are even justified or appropriate with regard to the international law of war.

There are certain principles on the basis of which we could claim that the legal regulation of cyberwarfare is appropriate from the perspective of classic warfare. Any variation or deviation from these principles means a breach of international law, regardless of whether they occur in the real or virtual environment. The fundamental international acts falling within the scope of the law of war, which relate to the field of cyberwarfare, include (adapted from Darnton [DAR 06]):

– Discrimination: the legitimate use of military weapons and tactics must be discriminatory, i.e. it must distinguish between military and civilian targets. Indiscriminate war is illegal, although indirect damage to civilian targets is inevitable. Many scenarios of cyberwarfare violate the principle of discrimination as they present a threat mostly to civilian targets and civilian infrastructure.

– Proportionality: the use of military weapons and tactics must be proportionate to the military objectives. Many forms of cyberwarfare do not have a well-defined military target, which means they cannot be proportional.

– Legality: the use of military force should not be in contravention with the international law and international agreements. Examples of cyberwarfare most often do not violate the laws of war, but the international law concerning, for example, the interruption and disabling of communications.

– Necessity: the use of military force and tactics must be necessary to achieve the set goal, which is closely connected with the principle of proportionality. Since many actions of cyberwarfare do not have a well-defined objective, they thus cannot be necessary.

– Humanity: the use of military force should not cause unnecessary suffering to victims. This means that any weapon that causes consequences outside the place and time of a war zone is illegal. Many forms of cyberwarfare are not aimed at a specific war zone, which causes the spread of terror and fear.

– Neutrality: the use of military force should not cause any harm to people or their property in the neutral zones or countries, which are officially declared as neutral. Given the ubiquity of cyberwarfare, it is difficult to argue that to achieve its objectives it does not use facilities and infrastructure of neutral countries or causes them harm.

The explanation of these norms shows that the cases of cyberwarfare violate most of the basic principles of the law of war. So far, a case of cyberwarfare that would fit all of the above requirements has not been observed, because this would mean that, in order to be classified as a state of war in accordance with the norms of war, such a case of a cyberattack should be officially declared, precisely defined and targeted into specific targets of the war using urgent techniques and causing minimal damage. It is, thus, impossible to classify cyberwarfare as war in the true sense of the word, but as a specific, broader socially motivated crime.

In addition to the violations of international legal norms that deny the classification of cyberwarfare as a state of war, this cyber phenomenon also challenges the traditional concept of national security. Rawnsley [RAW 05] believes that the global flow of information is a non-military security issue that affects domestic and international policies, regardless of the political or geographical barriers and avoiding the core elements of state power. Cyberwarfare, thus, challenges the traditional concept of policies, which is based on the idea of formal autonomy and sovereignty, and draws attention to the fact that national security is no longer equated with state security. Even Jurich [JUR 08] argues that the adoption of relevant legislation is subject to the issue of the relationship between state sovereignty and the increasing dependence on ICT.

When taking this perspective, it is clear that cyberwarfare poses a serious challenge to the international law, but is still significantly different from conventional warfare. With the exception of some information operations, cyberwarfare constitutes operations that are not focused on the exact time or place of the event, as well as consequences that are not momentary, but mainly include interruptions of infrastructure, logistics and resources, as well as misinformation. Although the effects are not immediate, they can be as dangerous and harmful as conventional warfare [DAR 06]. The dilemma whether cyberwarfare poses serious consequences, similar to conventional warfare, since its method of operation seriously breaches the applicable international rules of war, remains unresolved. In addition, it changes traditional concepts of national security and sovereignty, as it operates in a completely new environment, which has not been anticipated from the legislative point of view. Apart from this dilemma, which prevents the proper classification of warfare in the cyber environment, there are also other problems that emphasize the incompetence of regulation and the solving of this kind of crime to an even greater extent.

The first problem relates to the field of defining the powers of the authorities in the cyber environment. Cybercrime, by which cyberwarriors achieve set goals, operates in an international cyber environment in which national borders are not outlined, and the perpetrators usually originate from foreign countries. Every individual, department or organization present in cyberspace must take care of their own protection and define the limits of (un)permitted access; however, due to their lack of willingness, this is more often an exception than the rule. Therefore, how is it possible to argue that an individual is located in the U.S. or in the Chinese cyberspace, if these environments are not defined, the servers and networks are increasingly intertwined and entering them is relatively easy? The international law gives each country the right to freedom on their national territory. This principle suggests that each country has the right to autonomy, safety from violence and sovereignty on its national territory. No country is, thus, allowed to use its armed forces to invade the territory of another country via sea, air or land. Therefore, the principle of state sovereignty in cyberspace is questionable [JOY 11]. The best solution in the drafting of cyberwarfare regulatory frameworks was provided by the United Nations. The Charter of the United Nations[63] (hereinafter "the UN Charter") [UNI 45] simply stipulates that all member states engaging in international relations must refrain from the threat or use of force against the territorial integrity or political independence of another

---

63 Three fundamental interests of the UN Charter: (1) international security and peace, (2) international human rights and fundamental freedoms, (3) economic and social development.

country[64], but in spite of that the problem of understanding cyberspace is still not resolved. Although law enforcement authorities physically protect our territory, the question of who actually protects cyberspace arises. Given the lack of will and understanding, as well as the absence of legislative regulations, we can justifiably claim that the answer is no one.

The second problem associated with cyberwarfare and its legal basis relates to the detection and identification of individual cases of cybercrime as a political, ideological or business case of a carefully planned fight for information. The Convention is the only legally binding international instrument, which relates only to crime associated with computers, and computer, information and communication systems. Flexible definitions provided by the Convention allow signatories to develop national legislation in accordance with their unique social views on crime, but inconsistent standards prevent adequate international regulation [JUR 08]. Joyner and Lotrionte [JOY 01] argue that it is difficult to prove the motive and purpose of a certain country due to the techniques[65] and nature of intrusions, while Bratusa [BRA 11] believes that this situation deprives countries of the possibility to actively respond to the cyberattacks of another country, because they cannot ascertain that in a particular case they are dealing with the systematic demolition of their information systems. Therefore, no distinction is made between errors, criminal

---

64 Articles 2(4) (use of force) and 51 (right of self-defense) of the UN Charter constitute the fundamental framework for the study of violence and tension in the international environment.

65 To ensure the most rational use of resources, servers automatically lead information through a variety of network channels to avoid congestion. A regular user of the Internet who is located in the United States and requests information from a server in France, transfers such a request through a number of different servers that are in its path. Due to such processes, it is difficult to trace the source of the request, especially if the signal was deliberately routed through various servers around the world [JUR 08].

offence of intrusion into the information system and the declaration of war by a certain country.

The example of various scenarios judged according to the criteria of the Convention demonstrates the inadequacy of the current normative regulation and the inability of countries and their authorities in investigating and prosecuting the problems related to cyberwarfare. In the first situation, a virus is created and dispatched by an individual. In the second situation, perpetrators involve a group of civilian individuals who act only within the territory of their own country. The third situation represents a group of criminals consisting of citizens of different countries, whereas the only one who is present in the country is the author of the virus. Although the Convention predicts or governs the first two scenarios, and provides for the criminal responsibility of individuals, it fails to do so in the third scenario and relies only on international cooperation. In this case, a country – the victim – has to assent to the sanctions that are imposed by individual countries, and hope that the involved country will use a fair punishment for its citizens – the perpetrators [JUR 08]. According to Shackelford [SHA 09], the disclosure of perpetrators in the context of dealing with cybercrime and the corroboration of guilt or the investigation and prosecution of perpetrators, should be considered by defining a certain (low) degree of probability in the legal regime, especially due to specific problems stemming from cybercrime, i.e. the anonymity afforded by cyberspace.

The third problem associated with inadequate legal regulation refers to the gathering of evidence and conducting investigations at the national and organizational level. Despite the fact that laws define the importance of evidence in electronic form, in practice, law enforcement authorities are still faced with the problem related to the lack of understanding of digital forensic processes, which increases doubts about the reliability of evidence and possibilities for challenging their credibility. Due to the transnational nature of this type of crime, law enforcement authorities are heavily dependent on the assistance of foreign countries during their investigation. The Convention also identifies the need for mutual cooperation on the basis of requests or bilateral treaties and agreements on mutual assistance. At present, the situation is such that the possibilities of transferring responsibilities and feigning ignorance are still common. Moreover, the current legislation regarding the protection of personal data prevents government authorities from examining Internet traffic at points of entry into their country, which means that the current legal regulations represent a major limitation. There are similar problems even at the organizational level. When a suspicion arises that employees are performing industrial espionage, companies mostly do not have any legal basis allowing for the transfer of personal belongings (e.g. USB sticks and other storage devices) or for gaining access to the content on their computer at work (e.g. e-mail and other storage options available online or on a certain part of the Internet network). This can only be done by a competent authority in cases where an investigation of the suspicion of a criminal act is initiated. This is a sensitive and urgent topic from the standpoint of workers' supervision and their workplace privacy. It is interesting to note that such limitations are mostly observed in the wider European area, while in countries where cyberwarfare is very extensive (e.g. the United States and China), the concept of employees' privacy is strongly subordinate to the interests and needs of employers. Insight into employees' work habits and activities (including in the field of ICT) is quite common in these countries.

This is closely linked with a problem relating to the possibility of reaction or response by a country to a hostile attack. The Convention should identify response options of the attacked country acting in self-defense, which would enable it to prevent attacks on its systems. The UN Charter provides each country with the right to defense, which also applies to cyberattacks. However, the possibility of a counterattack only applies to self-defense in the event that an attack is underway. In legal terms, countries do not have the right to use force in defense and such an attack on an information system is understood in a similar way to espionage. The use of force to retaliate is therefore not allowed.

Prohibitions of the UN Charter determine exceptions, since Article 51 recognizes the right of individual or collective self-defense in case of an armed attack on a UN member until the Security Council decides on the measures necessary to ensure international peace and security. However, the right to self-defense is limited to the response to an armed attack; the action under this restriction is narrower than the concept of the "use of force", which is forbidden by Article 2(4) of the Charter. This means that a country can become a victim of the "use of force", which is not classified as an armed attack, and therefore has no right to self-defense [JUR 08]. In the event of a cyberattack on the network, a country (victim) can react in self-defense (reasonable, proportionate and necessary measures to protect its own safety) as defined by Article 2(4) only if the attack would reach the level of an armed conflict, which means that it must produce the same consequences. If a cyberattack does not occur in parallel or before the conventional military attack, Article 2(4) can only be taken into account if the purpose of such a cyberattack was to cause physical damage and destruction [SHA 09].

NATO, the largest international security organization, which found out how important cooperation and international assistance are in cases of cyberthreats only during the information conflict between Russia and Estonia, came across a similar problem. The attack on Estonia's information systems fell within the scope of Article 5 of the North Atlantic Treaty [NOR 49], which states that an attack on a NATO member state obliges the alliance to counterattack the aggressor. In the history of NATO, the attack on Estonia was the first case in which a member state requested NATO assistance to protect its own digital assets [HUG 09]. NATO security specialists were dispatched to Tallinn (capital of Estonia), but could not provide assistance, because the Internet in Estonia is managed by international organizations and private companies [TAN 08]. This showed the weakness of the NATO doctrine and strategy [HUG 09]. After that, NATO took a step forward in strengthening the alliance in this area for the first time by issuing the Bucharest Summit Declaration [BUC 08], which in Article 47 stipulates that NATO is committed to protecting the information infrastructure of the alliance against cyberattacks and helping to counter such attacks. The Declaration also mentions the need for cooperation with individual countries and defines policies on cybersecurity. Following the adoption of this Declaration, the Cooperative CyberDefense Centre of Excellence (CCDCOE) was established in Estonia, which should employ experts from various countries. This is the 10th COE established by NATO, but the only one that deals exclusively with the response to cyberattacks. The second result of the Declaration was demonstrated through the establishment of the CDMA[66] in Brussels, which was NATO's attempt to centralize its cybersecurity capabilities (NATO Opens New Centre of Excellence on CyberDefense [NAT 08]). Its purpose is to bring public and private sectors together in the development of cybersecurity and safety measures in the event of attacks [GRA 08].

Dilemmas also arise in the field of human rights protection, as the law relating to this area states that each individual has the right to physical privacy, personal data privacy, privacy regarding communications and space, and freedom from surveillance. Privacy is also very important when using the Internet. Countries and hackers can mask their identity in the management of cyberspace and thus

---

66 CyberDefense Management Authority.

jeopardize the privacy of other, innocent users. Just as countries have the right to hide behind the anonymous mask in cyberspace when carrying out cyberattacks, they also have the possibility of hacking into personal privacy under the pretext that this is necessary for the provision of cybersecurity. The coordination between national interests and human rights is and will continue to be a major challenge [SHA 09].

Problems associated with detecting, investigating and corroborating cases of cyberwarfare are widespread and very present. The current situation shows that international communities and individual countries do not focus enough attention on this threat, which is most often the result of misunderstanding and a false sense of security. Countries, cyberwarriors, who at the moment dictate the guidelines of cyberwarfare, are well aware of this, but the regulation of cyberwarfare can cause them more harm than good. What, therefore, can organizations and countries actually do in the current situation?

2.8. Defense against cyberwarfare

It is essential to adopt a universal international definition of cybercrime, so that experts and law enforcement agencies will be aware of the scope of the problem that they are fighting. It is also necessary to precisely define the (un) permitted methods of ICT use in the event of offensive and defensive operations carried out by countries and organizations. Specific forms of cybercrime, as well as politically, ideologically or economically motivated examples of information warfare have to be limited and defined, so that law enforcement authorities are able to thoroughly investigate cases. It is essential to define the permissible information operations in the event of offensive and defensive operations carried out by countries, and to collect data in cyberspace in order to enable an effective defense. At the same time, it is necessary to introduce international guidelines into national laws and thus contribute to the international harmonization of the use of technology permitted.

It is certainly necessary to adopt appropriate national security strategies, which should, in addition to other spatial domains that are critical to national security, also expose the cyberdomain as such. Due to its specific problems, it would be best to regulate cyberspace in a special national security strategy designed solely for the comprehensive regulation of cybersecurity. The authors would recommend considering the U.S. National Strategy to Secure Cyberspace [USC 03], which identifies the following three main objectives:

– prevention of cyberattacks on critical infrastructure;

– reducing vulnerability in case of cyberattacks;

– minimizing the effects and recovery time after the attack.

The Strategy also highlights the following basic measures that are necessary to establish an appropriate level of cybersecurity at the national level:

– the establishment of a national system for responding to cyber threats,

– national program to reduce cyber threats and risks,

– a program to raise national cybersecurity awareness,

– the establishment of government cyberspace protection,

– international cooperation for the achievement of national and cybersecurity.

It may be relevant to rely on the latest document adopted by the EU, entitled *Cybersecurity Strategy of the European Union: An Open, Safe and Secure Cyberspace* (hereinafter the Strategy; [CSE 13]), which highlights the following priority areas for the defense of cyberspace:

– achieving cyberresilience;

– drastically reducing cybercrime;

– developing a cyberdefense policy and capabilities related to the Common Security and Defence Policy (CSDP);

– developing industrial and technological resources for cybersecurity;

– establishing a coherent international cyberspace policy for the European Union and promoting core EU values.

The EU member states will transpose the guidelines of the Strategy into their national law, but these guidelines can also contribute to the drafting of global guidelines for the protection of cyberspace. Due to the increasing number of cyber threats, it is definitely necessary to protect the IT infrastructure as quickly as possible and thus set a good example for the organizational sphere. Accountability and qualitative protection must become top priorities (e.g. in 2010, it became mandatory to adjust the American electrical industry to the exact safety standards set by the NERC[67] organization).

In terms of the adoption and development of legislation, the authors agree with Jurich [JUR 08], who proposes the inclusion of non-state actors or the use of the "bottom-up law making process", which can identify and respect the factors required by the private sector that were overlooked by individual countries. The creation of a legal basis should, in his view, include representatives of smaller interest groups from different fields. By doing so, countries would, in addition to respecting the principle of better regulation, receive increased access to information about the latest technology, which can trigger proactive discussion, cooperation and information sharing.

---

67 North American Electric Reliability Corporation's Critical Infrastructure Protection.

After the adoption of appropriate strategies at the national level, it is also necessary to regulate the international level. Cybercrime and, in particular, cyberwarfare are highly international in nature, which is why national legislation and regulation alone are not sufficient. Shakelford [SHA 10] proposes the adoption of a multilateral agreement on cybersecurity to determine when a cyberattack can turn into an armed attack, which law should be applicable in the case of cyberwarfare and which response measures should follow. He also proposes the establishment of an international CERT with the relevant skills to respond to cyberattacks and to investigate incidents by identifying the perpetrators. This could also be done with the association of all CERTs around the world within the NATO Center in Estonia.

If they wish to prevent attacks on their own critical information structure, individual countries must eliminate certain statutory limitations, which currently represent an obstacle because of the desire to protect individual privacy and personal data in cyberspace. By all means, it does not suffice to merely adopt and adapt legislation; the society has to learn about the prevalence and severity of the problem, law enforcement agencies have to be trained appropriately and encouraged in their participation at local and global levels. In the phase of the investigation and detection of cybercrime, the competent authorities must also take into account the possibility of a cyberattack carried out by another country or group and refocus their attention on determining motives for attacks. The cooperation between states and government departments is essential, and the pursuit of this objective, therefore, requires the strengthening of international relations by concluding bilateral and multilateral agreements on mutual assistance and cooperation.

To ensure capabilities for the investigation of cyberwarfare cases efficiently, a precise definition of responsibilities for providing protection is also required. It must be determined who is responsible for the protection of the entire IT infrastructure, what organizations' roles are and how countries can improve their protection. Siroli [SIR 06] believes that until now the defense and protection fell within the competence of the government, but today this is no longer feasible. The private sector cannot fully rely on the protection provided by military forces. Due to new circumstances, the private infrastructure owners must play a key role in protecting their own equipment from abuse, intrusions and external attacks.

Organizations, especially those that operate with systems that are crucial for the normal functioning of society, must certainly provide for adequate security and protection at the micro level by themselves. They can achieve this by raising the level of business ethics and safety awareness among employees, users, business partners, customers and especially the management, which is actually responsible for the state of morale and security in a certain organization. Adequate safety data classification and restrictions regarding the number of people with access to such data is a necessary step, which, together with appropriate security clearance of persons who enter the physical space or cyberspace of a certain organization, helps to prevent many risks and realized threats. Above all, it is necessary to implement the recommendations and standards at national and organizational levels, which are used to effectively carry out a thorough analysis of the information system, to identify key types of vulnerabilities and the most salient points, and to introduce the necessary security mechanisms. This is the only way to ensure an effective policy of continuous operation, which is the primary goal of any organization and country.

To establish the protection or cybersecurity against cases of cyberwarfare, Knapp and Boulton [KNA 06] provide two strategies that, when applied together, are proven to be effective:

– The architectural strategy proposes setting up multiple layers of protection, which increases the time and effort invested by malicious attackers who want to break into the system and have to overcome many obstacles. Every single obstacle does not provide sufficient protection, but in relation to each other (e.g. multiple firewalls and antivirus software in combination with the detection of unauthorized entries) represents a comprehensive measure.

– The managerial strategy proposes the employment of certified safety managers and qualified personnel, as well as the implementation of risk analysis, and tracking trends in risk management policies.

When planning and implementing measures to restore information security, it is beneficial to understand and follow the guidelines of situational prevention. Perpetrators of crime in cyberspace pursue the same objectives and operate under the same influences as the perpetrators of traditional forms of crime. Undoubtedly, the environment in which the perpetrator acts is an important factor of crime. The characteristics of cyberspace, in which an offense takes place, are extremely varied. Security measures taken by organizations or countries at the entry points into their own IT environment certainly affect the decision of the offender. The architectural strategy is thus a very appropriate measure to deter malicious users of ICT. The greater the effort the offender must invest, and the longer the time that must be spent to overcome security obstacles, the less likely it is for the offender to decide to carry out a criminal act. Mesko [MES 02] states that an environment where there is a high risk of arrest and where it is not easy to obtain the proceeds will have a preventive effect, which is also recognized by the authors of the previously presented study on the cost of cybercrime [AND 12]. Therefore, organizations and countries must invest in the establishment of a multifaceted strategy for information security. The higher the number of protective mechanisms that overlap and prevent the perpetrator's unauthorized access to the system, the lower the likelihood that the offender will decide to invade. The combination of the quantity and quality of the measures is, of course, very important. It is the perpetrator, who we wish to influence by changing cyberspace. The best solution for the prevention of cybercrime is to extend the perpetrator's time and effort needed to achieve their goal and to adopt relevant legislation, which increases the chance of detection and conviction of offenders.

2.9. Cyberwarfare conclusion

The comprehensive protection of information infrastructure also depends on the awareness and responsibility of each individual using ICT. All users connected to the global network are potential victims of the malicious exploitation of information assets, and can quickly become cyberwarriors. Education on information security is, therefore, an inevitable step in learning, in understanding and in the internalization of responsibility in a digital environment. Each individual is responsible for their own actions in any environment, and it is up to countries and organizations to make society aware of the risks associated with networks that are part of our everyday lives.

When discussing the issues connected with cyberwarfare, we should be aware that the benefits arising from the use of ICT and cyberspace prevail over the disadvantages arising from the threat posed by their use. It is of vital importance for countries to set an example to organizations and for international organizations to act as role models for local entities. It is difficult to expect that other countries will refrain from developing methods and theories that are developed and used by global superpowers.

Apart from the previously mentioned proposals and measures, it is primarily necessary to understand the nature of cyberwarfare in order to regulate existing problems. It is, therefore, necessary to determine the presence and degree of prevalence of this phenomenon in the organizational and national spheres. Facts are the only elements that can support and help the planning of necessary protective and preventive measures. Research into cyberwarfare must cover the perception of this phenomenon in organizational and national environments to determine the level of its use, legitimacy and prevalence. In addition, an agreement at the national and global levels needs to be reached on the scope of this phenomenon, on what constitutes criminal acts and on how to respond to an attack, and appropriate measures have to be taken on the basis of relevant, internationally accepted legal bases.

Conclusion

In terms of cybersecurity, the future is the most important time dimension. With respect to ensuring safety and eliminating threats, the activities undertaken in the present and the past are already too late; hence, it is necessary to focus on the analysis of potential risks and opportunities that will occur in the future. This book demonstrates that the existence of cybercrime is an indisputable fact. At the moment, cybercrime development and its threat to cyberspace users are increasing exponentially. It is also known that cybercrime is expanding its range of operation and attracting ever more organized, sophisticated and covert perpetrators within its environment. Due to their political, economic or ideological motivations, these people represent the greatest threat to society because the societal consequences of their actions are much more detrimental than the consequences of traditional, financially motivated cybercrime. In this context, it is clear that the perpetrators of criminal acts are not inactive, but are extremely up-to-date, flexible, adaptable and organized. It is precisely these attributes that law enforcement agencies, legislative acts, organizations and countries should possess when encountering threats in cyberspace. However, the current situation shows that the opposite holds true.

Outdated, rigid and fragmented legislation prevents development and the proper course of action being undertaken by competent authorities and victims in the event of executed security attacks. In general, the legal basis is a compulsory step that has to be taken before implementing any restrictive and preventive measures in cyberspace. Due to the organized and transnational nature of cybercrime, the homogeneity or harmonization of national laws at the international level is also a necessary prerequisite for the ultimate success of criminal proceedings and the prosecution of perpetrators. The adoption of such legislation is impossible due to inadequate understanding of both individual cyber threats and those that are most dangerous to the society.

The lack of universal definitions and consensus on the definition of certain concepts alone indicates that those fighting against cybercrime are lagging behind its perpetrators. How could we eliminate something that does not even exist or that we cannot understand? In order to determine which elements require urgent responses, it is necessary to perform an analysis of the national infrastructure and the very perception of cybercrime in the society. Which are the most dangerous and the most common threats? What is their definition? Which legal acts are already regulating them? What are the risks for a country and which consequences these might produce? Am I a target of cyberwarfare? Can I experience a cyberterrorist attack? These and similar questions need to be posed to the users of information and communication technologies (ICT) who form an information network, which is the main target of the perpetrators. It will only be possible to determine which are the most urgent steps that need to be taken by first providing answers to such dilemmas, challenges and uncertainties. This is the only path toward understanding the nature and foundations of cybercrime.

The future will be characterized by further development of cybercrime techniques; however, the question is whether those who are at risk will also experience such development? At the moment, safety and protection lie in the hands of individuals, while in the governments' perspective, the cyber environment is characterized by a relatively anarchic state due to a lack of awareness. In order to regulate such a disorder and increase (global, national and individual) information security, much more will have to be done than merely providing warnings, education and awareness, which have been constantly emphasized. Tangible activities, fieldwork, examination, analysis and evaluation, as well as the implementation of measures, will be needed in order to determine the current state of security and risk. By establishing protection at national or social levels, organizations or individuals are actually not doing anything for themselves. Until the adoption of obligatory standards and relevant legislation, as well as the achievement of a common understanding of cybersecurity issues, there is essentially nothing to rely on.

The future is here, and it requires that the participation of different actors, professionals and especially all interest groups be included in the plans for the development of cybersecurity strategies today.

Bibliography

[ABU 13] ABU AMER A., "Israel braces for cyberwarfare with Palestinians", *Almonitor*, 2013. Available at http://www.al-monitor. com/pulse/originals/2013/02/israel-palestine-cyber-war.html.

[ALB 06] ALBERTS D.S., GARSTKA J.J., STEIN F.P., *Network Centric Warfare: Developing and Leveraging Information Superiority*, DoD Command and Control Research Program, Washington, 2006.

[ALE 11] ALEXANDER K.B., "Warfighting in cyberspace", *Military Technology*, vol. 3, no. 1, pp. 41–45, 2011.

[ALP 11] ALPEROVITCH D., *Revealed: Operation Shady RAT*, McAffe, 2011. Available at http://blogs.mcafee.com/mcafee-labs/revealed-operation-shady-rat.

[ALS 05] ALSHALAN A., "Cyber-crime fear and victimization: an analysis of a national survey", 2005. Available at http://www.cse.msstate.edu/~dampier/study%20materials/Natio nalCrimeStats.pdf.

[AND 08] ANDERSON K., "Hacktivism and politically motivated computer crime", 2008. Available at http://www. aracnet.com/~kea/Papers/Politically%20Motivated%20Compute r%20Crime.pdf.

[AND 12] ANDERSON R., BARTON C., BOEHME R., *et al.*, "Measuring the cost of cybercrime", *11th Annual Workshop on the Economics of Information Security (WEIS 2012)*, 2012. Available at weis2012.econinfosec.org/papers/Anderson_ WEIS2012.pdf .

[ARM 04] ARMISTEAD L., *Information Operations: Warfare and the Hard Reality of Soft Power*, Brassey's Inc., Washington, 2004.

[BAS 10] BASKERVILLE R., "Third-degree conflicts: information warfare", *European Journal of Information Systems*, vol. 19, no. 1, pp. 1–4, 2010.

[BBC 07] BBC NEWS, "Estonia hit by 'Moscow cyber war'", *BBC News*, 2007. Available at http://news.bbc.co.uk/2/hi/europe/6665145.stm.

[BBC 11] BBC NEWS TECHNOLOGY, "Internet explorer story was bogus", *BBC News Technology*, 2011. Available at http://www.bbc.co.uk/news/technology-14389430.

[BER 74] BERGIER J., *Vohunstvo V Industriji In Znanosti*, Mladinska knjiga, Ljubljana, 1974.

[BER 03] BERKOWITZ B., *The New Face of War: How War Will Be Fought in the 21st Century*, Simon & Schuster Inc., New York, 2003.

[BER 11a] BERNIK I., PRISLAN K., *"Proces upravljanja s tveganji v informacijski varnosti"*, in PAVŠIČ M.T. (ed.), 11. slovenski dnevi varstvoslovja, Fakulteta za varnostne vede, Ljubljana, 2011. Available at http://www.fvv.uni-mb.si/dv2010/zbornik/informacijska_varnost/Bernik_Prislan%20proces%20upravljanj a.pdf.

[BER 11b] BERNIK I., MESKO G., "Internetna študija poznavanja kibernetskih groženj in strahu pred kibernetsko kriminaliteto", *Revija za kriminalistiko in kriminologijo*, vol. 62, no. 3, pp. 242–252, 2011.

[BET 06] BETZ D.J., LEE S., "Information in the Western way of warfare: too much of a good thing?", *Pacific Focus*, vol. 21, no. 2, pp. 197–231, 2006.

[BEZ 09] BEZLOVA A., "China's modern muscle on parade", *Asia Times Online*, 2009. Available at http://www.atimes.com/atimes/China/KA24Ad02.html.

[BRA 11] BRATUSA T., *Asimetrično Bojevanje In Strategija Posrednega Nastopanja V Kibernetski Vojni*, Fakulteta za varnostne vede, Ljubljana, 2011.

[BUC 08] BUCHAREST SUMMIT DECLARATION, NATO, 2008. Available at http://www.nato.int/cps/en/natolive/official_texts_8443.htm.

[BUL 10] BULGURCU B., CAVUSOGLU H., BENBASAT I., "Information security policy compliance: an numerical study of rational-based beliefs and information security awereness", *MIS Quarterly*, vol. 34, no. 3, pp. 523–A7, 2010.

[CHI 09] CHIESA R., DUCCI S., CIAPPI S., *Profiling Hackers. The Science of Criminal Profiling as Applied to the World of Hacking*, Auerbach Publications, New York, 2009

[CHU 13] CHUNG C., "War with Iran: US and Israel cyber warfare against Iran is very much underway", *Policymic*, 2013. Available at http://www.policymic.com/articles/21694/war-with-iran-us-and-israel-cyber-warfare-against-iran-is-very-much-underway.

[CIV 08] CIVIL.GE., "S.Ossetian news sites hacked", *Civil.Ge*, 2008. Available at http://www.civil.ge/eng/article.php?id=18896.

[COC 01] CONVENTION ON CYBERCRIME, "Convention on cybercrime", 2001. Available at http://conventions.coe.int/Treaty/en/Treaties/Html/185.htm

[COC 09] COCKCROFT T., Late modernity, risk and the construction of fear of crime", in MESKO G., COCKCROFT T., CRAWFORD A., LEMAITRE A. (eds), *Crime, Media and Fear of Crime*, Tipografija, Ljubljana, pp. 13–26, 2009.

[COE 03] COUNCIL OF EUROPE, "Additional protocol to the convention on cybercrime, concerning the criminalisation of acts of a racist and xenophobic nature committed through computer systems", Council of Europe, 2003. Available at http://conventions.coe.int/Treaty/en/Treaties/Html/189.htm.

[COE 10] COUNCIL OF EUROPE, "Convention on cybercrime CETS No.: 185", 2010. Available at http://conventions.coe.int/Treaty/Commun/ChercheSig.asp?NT=185&CM=8&DF=28/10/2010&CL=ENG.

[COH 13a] COHEN G., "IDF forms new force to combat cyber warfare", *Haaretz*, 2013. Available at http://www.haaretz.com/news/diplomacy-defense/idf-forms-new-force-to-combat-cyber-warfare.premium-1.506979.

[COH 13b] COHEN G., YARON O., "Barak acknowledges Israel's cyber offensive for first time", *Haaretz*, 2013. Available at http://www. haaretz.com/news/diplomacy-defense/barak-acknowledges-israel-s-cyber-offensive-for-first-time-1.434767?block=true.

[COL 08] COLEMAN K., "Cyber-attacks and cyber-disasters: are you prepared?", *TechNewsWorld*, 2008. Available at http://www.technewsworld.com/story/62725.html?wlc=1317055553.

[CON 09] CONNOLLY K., "Germany accuses China of industrial espionage", *The Guardian*, 2009. Available at http://www.guardian.co.uk/world/2009/jul/22/germany-china-industrial-espionage.

[CON 13] CONSTANTIN L., "Researchers discover new global cyber-espionage campaign", *Info World*, 2013. Available at http://www.infoworld.com/d/security/researchers-discover-new-global-cyber-espionage-campaign-213614.

[CSE 13] CYBERSECURITY STRATEGY OF THE EU, *Cybersecurity Strategy of the European Union: An Open, Safe and Secure Cyberspace*, European Commission, 2013. Available at http://ec.europa.eu/information_society/newsroom/cf/dae/document.cfm?doc_id=1667.

[CYB 11] CYBER WARFARE, *Tech-FAQ*, 2011. Available at http://www.tech-faq.com/cyber-warfare.html.

[CYB 13] CYBERSPACE, *Cyberspace*, 2013. Available at http://www.webopedia.com/TERM/C/cyberspace.html.

[DAL 11] DALAL P., "Cyber warfare policy of India. International ICT policies and strategies", 2011. Available at http://ictps.blogspot.com/2011/06/cyber-warfare-policy-of-india.html.

[DAR 06] DARNTON G., "Information warfare and the laws of war", in HALPIN E., TREVORROW P., WEBB D., WRIGHT S. (eds), *Cyberwar, Netwar and the Revolution in Military Affairs*, Palgrave Macmillan, New York, pp. 139–153, 2006.

[D'AR 09] D'ARCY J., HOVAN A., GALLETTA D., "User awareness of security countermeasures and its impact on information systems misuse: a deterrence approach", *Information Systems Research*, vol. 20, no. 1, pp. 79–98, 2009.

[DAV 07] DAVIS J., "Hackers take down the most wired country in Europe", *Wired Magazine*, 2007. Available at http://www.wired.com/politics/security/magazine/15-09/ff_estonia.

[DEM 03] DEMETRIOU C., SILKE A., "A criminological internet "Sting": experimental evidence of illegal and deviant visits to a website trap", *The British Journal of Criminology*, vol. 43, no. 1, pp. 213–222, 2003.

[DET 11] DETICA, "Detica and office of cyber security and information assurance. The cost of cyber crime, cybercrime 2011", *Detica*, 2011. Available at https://www.gov.uk/government/uploads/system/uploads/attachment_data/file/60943/the-cost-of-cyber-crime-full-report.pdf.

[DIM 10] DIMC M., DOBOVSEK B., "Perception of cyber crime in Slovenia", *Varstvoslovje*, vol. 12, no. 4, pp. 378–396, 2010.

[DIO 11] DION M., "Corruption, fraud and cybercrime as dehumanizing phenomena", *International Journal of Social Economics*, vol. 38, no. 5, pp. 466–476, 2011.

[DIR 95] DIRECTIVE 95/46/, European Parliament and of the Council, 1995. Available at http://eur-lex.europa.eu/LexUriServ/LexUriServ.do?uri=CELEX:31995L0046:en:HTML.

[DMC 98] DMCA, "The Digital Millennium Copyright Act Of 1998", *U.S. Copyright Office Summary*, 1998. Available at http://www.copyright.gov/legislation/dmca.pdf.

[DOB 09] DOBOVSEK B., *Transnacionalna Kriminaliteta*, Fakulteta za varnostne vede, Ljubljana, 2009.

[EC3 13] EC3, European CyberCrime Centre, 2013. Available at https://www.europol.europa.eu/ec3.

[ECO 07] EUROPEAN COMMISSION, "Towards a general policy on the fight against cyber crime", May 2007. COM(2007) 267 final, 2007. Available at http://eur-lex.europa.eu/LexUriServ/LexUriServ.do?uri=CELEX:52007DC0267:EN:NOT.

[ELL 10] ELLIS-CHRISTENSEN T., "What is industrial espionage?", 2010. Available at http://www.wisegeek.com/what-is-industrial-espionage.htm.

[ENI 08] ENISA, "Security economics and the internal market", 2008. Available at http://www.enisa.europa.eu/publications/archive/economics-sec/at_download/fullReport.

[ERI 06] ERIKSSON J., GIACOMELLO G., "The information revolution, security, and international relations: (IR) relevant theory?", *International Political Science Review*, vol. 27, no. 3, pp. 221–244, 2006.

[EUR 07] EUROPOL, "High tech crimes within the EU: old crimes new tools, new crimes new tools. Threat Assessment 2007", *High Tech Crime Centre*, 2007. Available at http://www.enisa.europa.eu/activities/cert/events/files/ENISA_Europol_threat_assessment_2007_Dileone.pd.

[EVA 09] EVANS K., CAREY R.J., "Success in national cyberdefense", *IT Professional*, vol. 11, no. 5, pp. 42–43, 2009.

[FBI 11] FBI, "Cyber crime", 2011. Available at http://www.fbi.gov/about-us/investigate/cyber/cyber.

[FED 13] FEDERATION OF AMERICAN SCIENTISTS, "Echelon", 2013. Available at http://www.fas.org/irp/program/process/echelon.htm.

[FIN 08] FINJAN, "Web security trends report", Finjan Malicious Code Research Center, 2008. Available at http://www.cittadininternet.org/UserFiles/File/Fatti%20importanti_Italia/Trend_Report_Q2_2008.pdf.

[FRI 08] FRITZ J., "How China will use cyber warfare to leapfrog in military competitiveness", *Culture Mandala*, vol. 8, no. 1, pp. 28–80, 2008.

[FUL 09] FULLBROOK M., "Tips on stamping out data leakage & industrial espionage during recession", ICT Review: Computer Hardware and Software Review Journal, 2009. Available at http://ictreview.blogspot.com/2009/03/tips-on-stamping-out-dataleakage.

[FUR 04] FURNELL S.M., WARREN, M.J., "Computer hacking and cyber terrorism: the real threats in the new millennium", in O'DAY A. (ed.), *Cyberterrorism*, Ashgate Publishing Limited, Aldershot, pp. 111–117, 2004.

[GAO 07] GAO-07-705, "Cybercrime public and private entities face challenges in addressing cyber threats. U.S. Government Accountability Office", 2007. Available at http://www.gao.gov/new.items/d07705.pdf.

[GAR 11] GARTNER GROUP, "Security risk management", 2011. Available at http://www.gartner.com/technology/research/security-risk-management.jsp.

[GOO 10] GOODCHILD J., "Social engineering: the basics", 2010. Available at http://www.csoonline.com/article/514063/social-engineering-the-basics.

[GOR 11] GORMAN S., BARNES J.E., "Cyber combat: act of war", *The Wall Street Journal*, 2011. Available at http://online.wsj.com/article/SB10001424052702304563104576355623135782718.html.

[GRA 08] GRANT I., "Nato sets up cyber defence management authority in Brussels", *Computer Weekly.com*, 2008. Available at http://www.computerweekly.com/Articles/2008/04/04/230143/Nato-sets-up-Cyber-Defence-Management-Authority-in-Brussels.htm.

[GRA 10] GRADISAR M., LAMBERGER I., "Vpliv represivnih dejavnikov on zlorabe kreditnih in plačilnih kartic v Sloveniji", *Revija za kriminalistiko in kriminologijo*, vol. 61, no. 1, pp. 28–36, 2010.

[GRI 13] GRIMES R., "The cyber war is real – and our defenses are weak", *Info World*, 2013. Available at http://www.infoworld.com/d/security/the-cyber-war-real-and-our-defenses-are-weak-213016.

[HIG 08] HIGGINS K., "'Profiler' hacks global hacker culture", 2008. Available at http://www.darkreading.com/security/government/showArticle.jhtml?articleID=211201237.

[HIN 04] HINDE S., "Incalculable potential for damage by cyber-terrorism", in O'DAY A. (ed.), *Cyberterrorism*, Ashgate Publishing Limited, Aldershot, pp. 105–109, 2004.

[HIN 08] HINDUJA S., "Deindividuation and internet software piracy", *Cyberpsychology & Behavior*, vol. 11, no. 4, pp. 391–398, 2008.

[HUG 09] HUGHES R.B., "NATO and cyber defence: mission accomplished?", 2009. Available at http://www.atlcom.nl/ap_archive/pdf/AP%202009%20nr.%201/Hughes.pdf.

[IC3 10a] IC3, Internet crime report, Annual Report, NW3C – White Collar Crime Center, 2010. Available at http://www.ic3.gov/media/annualreport/2010_ic3report.pdf.

[IC3 10b] IC3, Internet crime report, 2010 Internet Crime Report, 2010. Available at http://ic3report.nw3c.org/docs/2010_IC3_Report_02_10_11_low_res.pdf.

[INT 12] INTERNET WORLD STATS, "Internet usage statistics", *Internet World Stats*, 2012. Available at http://www.internetworldstats.com/stats.htm.

[IOC 11] IOCTA, "EUROPOL public information. Internet facilitated organised crime", 2011. Available at https://www.europol.europa.eu/sites/default/files/publications/iocta.pdf.

[JOY 01] JOYNER C.C., LOTRIONTE C., "Information warfare as international coercion: elements of legal framework", *European Journal of International Law*, vol. 12, no. 5, pp. 825–865, 2001.

[JUR 08] JURICH J.P., "Cyber war and customary international law: the potential of a 'bottom up' approach to an international law of information opreations", *Chicago Journal of International Law*, vol. 9, no. 1, pp. 275–295, 2008.

[JWP 02] JOINT WARFARE PUBLICATION 3–80, "Information operations", 2002. Available at http://ics-www.leeds.ac.uk/papers/pmt/exhibits/2270/jwp3_80.pdf.

[KAB 98] KABAY M.E., "Anonymity and pseudonymity in cyberspace: deindividuation, incivility and lawlessness versus freedom and privacy", 1998. Available at http://www.egov.ufsc.br/portal/sites/default/files/anexos/2861-2855-1-PB.html.

[KAN 05] KANDUC Z., "Postmoderne nevarnosti, bojazni in 'dobri sovražniki'", *Revija za kriminalistiko in kriminologijo*, vol. 56, no. 4, pp. 337–347, 2005.

[KAU 13] KAUSHIK M., FITTER P.M., "Beware of the bugs. Can cyber attacks on India's critical infrastructure be thwarted?", *Business Today*, 2013. Available at http://business today.intoday.in/story/india-cyber-security-at-risk/1/ 191786.html.

[KIN 13] KINSELLA S., "The mountain of IP legislation – Mises economics blog", 2013. Available at http://archive.mises.org/ 14752/the-mountain-of-ip-legislation/.

[KNA 06] KNAPP K., BOULTON W.R., "Cyber-warfare threatens corporations: expansion into commercial environments", *Information Systems Management*, vol. 23, no. 2, pp. 76–87, 2006.

[KOV 07] KOVACIC M., "Direktor MI5 svari, da kitajski hekerji napadajo britanska podjetja", *Slo Tech*, 2007. Available at http://slo-tech.com/novice/t294715#crta.

[KRA 13] KRANE S., "Arab hackers attack the Jewish State", *ArutzSheva* 7, 2013. Available at http://www.israel nationalnews.com/News/News.aspx/160879#.UT-KktF35st.

[KRE 08] KREBS B., "Report: Russian hacker forums fueled Georgia cyber attacks", *Washington Post*, 2008. Available at http://voices.washingtonpost.com/securityfix/2008/10/report_rus sian_hacker_forums_f.html.

[LET 11] LETZING J., "DOJ, FBI disable massive 'botnet' attack", *The Wall Street Journal*, 2011. Available at http://www. marketwatch.com/story/doj-fbi-disable-massive-botnet-attack-2011-04-13.

[LEW 11] LEWIS L., "China's Blue Army of 30 computer experts could deploy cyber warfare on foreign powers", *AustralianIt*, 2011. Available at http://www.theaustralian.com.au/australian-it/ chinas-blue-army-could-conduct-cyber-warfare-on-foreign-powers/ story-e6frgakx-1226064132826.

[LEY 11] LEYDEN J., "UK finally ratifies cybercrime convention during Obama visit", *The Register*, 2011. Available at http://www.theregister.co.uk/2011/05/25/uk_ratifies_cybercrime _convention/.

[LOW 06] LOWENTHAL M.M., *Intelligence: From Secrets to Policy*, CQ Press, Washington, 2006.

[MAN 10] MANJIKIAN M.M., "From global village to virtual battlespace: the colonizing of the Internet and the extension of realpolitik", *International Studies Quarterly*, vol. 54, no. 2, pp. 381–401, 2010.

[MAN 11] MANDI M., "Google ameriškim oblastem izroča podatke o svojih evropskih uporabnikih", *Slo Tech*, 2011. Available at http://slo-tech.com/novice/t479187#crta.

[MAR 08] MARKOFF J., "Before the gunfire, cyberattacks", *The New York Times*, 2008. Available at http://www.nytimes.com/2008/08/13/technology/13cyber.html?_r=1&oref=slogin.

[MCC 05] MCCULLAGH A., CAELLI W., "Who goes there? Internet banking: a matter of risk and reward", in BOYD C., NIETO GONZALEZ J.M. (eds.), *Information Security and Privacy: 10th Australasian Conference*, ACISP 2005, Springer-Verlag, Berlin/Heidelberg, pp. 336–357, 2005.

[MCC 13] MCCAUL M., "Hardening our defenses against cyberwarfare", *The Wall Street Journal*, 2013. Available at http://online.wsj.com/article/SB10001424127887324662404578336862508763442.html.

[MES 00] MESKO G., "Miti o kriminaliteti v ZDA", *Revija za kriminalistiko in kriminologijo*, vol. 51, no. 4, pp. 305–313, 2000.

[MES 02] MESKO G., *Osnove Preprečevanja Kriminalitete*, Visoka policijsko varnostna šola, Ljubljana, 2002.

[MES 03] MESKO G., AREH I., "Strah pred kriminaliteto v urbanih okoljih", *Revija za kriminalistiko in kriminologijo*, vol. 54, no. 3, pp. 144–152, 2003.

[MES 06] MESKO G., PETROVEC D., AREH I., *et al.*, "Strah pred kriminaliteto v Sloveniji in Bosni in Hercegovini – izidi primerjalne študije", *Revija za kriminalistiko in kriminologijo*, vol. 57, no. 1, pp. 3–14, 2006.

[MES 08] MESKO G., SIFRER J., "Fear of crime in urban settings – an inquiry", *Varstvoslovje*, vol. 10, no. 4, pp. 550–560, 2008.

[MIL 11] MILLS E., "AntiSec hackers post stolen police data as revenge for arrests", *CNet News*, 2011. Available at http://news.cnet.com/8301-27080_3-20089054-245/antisec-hackers-post-stolen-police-data-as-revenge-for-arrests/.

[MIT 11] MITNICK K., *Ghost in the Wire*, Little, Brown and Company, New York, 2011.

[MOH 03] MOHAY G., ANDERSON A., BYRON C., DE VEL O., MCKEMMISH R., *Computer and Intrusion Forensic*, Artech House, Boston, 2003.

[MYA 10] MYANMAR TIMES, "Internet out-hits tourism sector", *Myanmar Times*, 2010. Available at http://www.mmtimes.com/2010/news/547/news54716.html.

[NAK 11] NAKASHIMA E., "Pentagon to outline cybersecurity strategy that offers more tools", *Washington Post*, 2011. Available on http://www.mailarchive.com/infowarrior@attrition.org/msg07585.html.

[NAR 11] NARAINE R., "Microsoft quietly finding, reporting security holes in Apple, Google products", *ZDNet*, 2011. Available at http://www.zdnet.com/blog/security/microsoft-quietly-finding-reporting-security-holes-in-apple-google-products/9319?tag=search-results-rivers;item8.

[NAT 08] NATO News, "NATO opens new centre of excellence on cyber defence", *NATO News*, 2008. Available at http://www.nato.int/docu/update/2008/05-may/e0514a.html.

[NEU 06] NEUMANN P.G., "Risk of computer-related technology", in HALPIN E., TREVORROW P., WEBB D., WRIGHT S. (eds), *Cyberwar, Netwar and the Revolution in Military Affairs*, Palgrave Macmillan, New York, pp. 72–81, 2006.

[NOR 49] NORTH ATLANTIC TREATY, NATO, 1949. Available at http://www.nato.int/cps/en/natolive/official_texts_17120.htm?selectedLocale=en.

[O'CO 11] O'CONNELL B., "FBI says white collar cyber crime tops 300,000 in '10", *Credit.com*, 2011. Available at http://www.credit.com/blog/2011/03/fbi-says-white-collar-cyber-crime-tops-300000-in-10/.

[O'GR 11] O'GRADY J.D., "AntiSec posts passwords from Apple survey server", *ZDNet*, 2011. Available at http://www.zdnet.com/blog/apple/antisec-posts-passwords-from-apple-survey-server-updated-5x/10498.

[PAU 11] PAULI D., "Chinese-built botnets full of bugs", *CRN*, 2011. Available at http://www.crn.com.au/News/275966,chinese-built-botnets-full-of-bugs.aspx.

[PER 09] PERSAK N., "Virtualnost, (ne)moralnost in škodljivost: normativna vprašanja nekaterih oblik kibernetične kriminalitete", *Revija za kriminalistiko in kriminologijo*, vol. 60, no. 3, pp. 191–198, 2009.

[POD 06] PODBREGAR I., "Some patterns of industrial espionage", *Varstvoslovje*, vol. 8, nos.3–4, pp. 323–331, 2006.

[POD 08] PODBREGAR I., *Vohunska dejavnost in gospodarstvo*, Fakulteta za varnostne vede, Ljubljana, 2008.

[PON 11] PONEMON INSTITUTE, *Second Annual Cost of Cyber Crime Study: Benchmark Study of U.S. Companies*, Ponemon Institute, Michigan, 2011.

[PON 12] PONEMON INSTITUTE, *2012 Cost of Cyber Crime Study: United States*, Ponemon Institute, Michigan, 2012. Available at http://www.ponemon.org/local/upload/file/2012_US_Cost_of_Cyber_Crime_Study_FINAL6%20.pdf.

[RAN 06] RANTAPELKONEN J., "Virtous virtual war", in HALPIN E., TREVORROW P., WEBB D., WRIGHT S. (eds), *Cyberwar, Netwar and the Revolution in Military Affairs*, Palgrave Macmillan, New York, pp. 51–71, 2006.

[RAS 11] RASHID F.Y., "Anonymous claims network breach of FBI security contractor ManTech", *eWeek*, 2011. Available at http://www.eweek.com/c/a/Security/Anonymous-Claims-Network-Breach-of-FBI-Security-Contractor-ManTech-693504/.

[RAW 05] RAWNSLEY G.D., "Old wine in new bottles: China–Taiwan computer-based 'information warfare' and propaganda", *International Affairs*, vol. 81, no. 5, pp. 1061–1078, 2005.

[RAY 11] RAYNER R., "Cyber war against Israel have taken very dangerous form", *The Hacker News*, 2011. Available at http://thehackernews.com/2011/08/cyber-war-against-israel-have-taken.html.

[RIC 07] RICHARDSON R., "CSI computer crime and security survey 2007", 2007. Available at http://i.cmpnet.com/v2.gocsi.com/pdf/CSISurvey2007.pdf.

[ROB 99] ROBINSON R.R., *Issues in Security Management; Thinking Criticaly About Security*, Butterworth, Woburn, 1999.

[ROC 08] ROCHE E. M., VAN NONSTRAND G., *Information Systems, Computer Crime & Criminal Justice*, Barraclough Ltd., CA, 2008.

[RUP 03] RUPNIK A., "Konvencija o kibernetski kriminaliteti, 'Budimpeštanska konvencija'", 2003. Available at http://www.ltfe.org/wp-content/pdf/Kiber_kriminaliteta.pdf.

[SAN 07] SANS INSTITUTE, "Corporate espionage 201", 2007. Available at http://www.sans.org/reading_room/whitepapers/engineering/corporate-espionage-201_512.

[SAN 11] SANGER D.E., "Pentagon to consider cyberattacks acts of war", *The New York Times*, 2011. Available at http://www.nytimes.com/2011/06/01/us/politics/01cyber.html?_r=0.

[SCH 03] SCHECHTER D., *Media Wars: News at a Time of Terror*, Rowman & Littlefield Publishers Inc., Lanham, 2003.

[SCI 10] SCIP, "Definition competitive intelligence", 2010. Available at http://competitive-intelligence.mirum.net/business-intelligence/definition-competitiveintelligence.html.

[SEA 10] SEARCH SECURITY, "Cyberwarfare", 2010. Available at http://searchsecurity.techtarget.com/definition/cyberwarfare.

[SEC 10] SECURITY THREAT REPORT, "Security threat report: mid-year", *Sophos*, 2010. Available at http://www.sophos.com/medialibrary/Gated%20Assets/white%20papers/sophossecuritythreatreportmidyear2010wpna.pdf.

[SHA 09] SHACKELFORD S.J., "From nuclear war to net war: analogizing cyber attacks in international law", *Berkley Journal of International Law*, vol. 25, no. 3, pp. 192–251, 2009.

[SHA 10] SHACKELFORD S.J., "Estonia three years later: a progress report on combating cyber attacks", *Journal of Internet Law*, vol. 13, no. 8, pp. 22–29, 2010.

[SIA 12] SIAVASH, "China cyber warriors: Blue Army", *CWZ Cybercrime*, 2012. Available at http://www.cyberwarzone.com/cyberwarfare/china-cyber-warriors-blue-army.

[SIN 11] SINGH K.G., "9/11 conspiracy: excuse for US reign of terror", *MWC News*, 2011. Available at http://mwcnews.net/focus/analysis/13432-us-reign-of-terror.html.

[SIR 06] SIROLI G.P., "Strategic information warfar: an introduction", in HALPIN E., TREVORROW P., WEBB D., WRIGHT S. (eds), *Cyberwar, Netwar and the Revolution in Military Affairs*, Palgrave Macmillan, New York, pp. 32–48, 2006.

[SLO 10] SLOCUM M., "Cyber warfare: don't inflate it, don't underestimate it", *O'Reilly Radar*, 2010. Available at http://radar.oreilly.com/2010/02/cyber-warfare-dont-inflate-it.html.

[SMI 10] SMITH S.E., "What is espionage?", 2010. Available at http://www.wisegeek.com/what-is-espionage.htm.

[SUP 11] SUPERVIZOR, "Spletna aplikacija za spremljanje javnih izdatkov", *Komisija za preprečevanje korupcije*, 2011. Available at http://supervizor.kpk-rs.si.

[TAN 08] TANNER J., "Stung by cyber warfare, Estonia, NATO allies to sign deal on cyber defense center", *Technology review*, 2008. Available at http://www.technologyreview.com/Wire/20770/.

[TAY 06] TAYLOR R.W., CAETI T.J., LOPER K., FRITSCH E.J., LIEDERBACH J.R., *Digital Crime and Digital Terrorism*, Prentice Hall, Upper Saddle River, 2006.

[THO 98] THOMAS T.I., "Russia's information warfare structures: understanding the roles of the security council, Fapsi, the state technical commission and the military", *European Security*, vol. 7, no. 1, pp. 156–156, 1998.

[TIW 11] TIWARY A.K., "Cyber warfare: the new threat", *Indian Defence Review*, 2011. Available at http://www.indiandefencereview.com/spotlights/cyber-warfare-the-new-threat/.

[TOD 08] TODAY.AZ., "Russian intelligence services undertook large scale attack against Day.Az server", *Today.Az*, 2008. Available at http://www.today.az/news/politics/46885.html.

[TOL 02] TOLLE G.A., "Shaping the information environment", *Military Review*, vol. 82, no. 3, pp. 47–49, 2002.

[TRA 07] TRAYNOR I., "Russia accused of unleashing cyberwar to disable Estonia", *The Guardian*, 2007. Available at http://www.guardian.co.uk/world/2007/may/17/topstories3.russia.

[TRI 94] TRIPS, "Agreement On trade-related aspects of intellectual property rights", *World Trade Organization*, 1994. Available at http://www.wto.org/english/docs_e/legal_e/27-trips.pdf.

[TRU 13] TRUSTWAVE, "Trustwave 2013 global security report", *Trustwave*, 2013. Available at http://www2.trustwave.com/rs/trustwave/images/2013-Global-Security-Report.pdf.

[UNI 04] UNITED NATIONS, "The COE international convention on cybercrime before its entry into force", 2004. Available at http://portal.unesco.org/culture/en/ev.php-URL_ID=19556&URL_DO=DO_TOPIC&URL_SECTION=201.html.

[UNI 45] UNITED NATIONS, "Charter of the United Nations", 1945. Available at http://www.un.org/en/documents/charter/intro.shtml, 1945.

[UNO 10] UNODC, "Cybercrime", 2010. Available at http://www.unodc.org/documents/data-and-analysis/tocta/10.Cybercrime.pdf.

[UPI 13] UPI.COM, "Iran builds up cyber warfare capabilities", *UPI.com*, 2013. Available at http://www.upi.com/Business_News/Security-Industry/2013/01/25/Iran-builds-up-cyber-warfare-capabilities/UPI-43931359145044/.

[USC 03] US-CERT, "National strategy to secure cyberspace", 2003. Available at http://www.us-cert.gov/reading_room/cyberspace_strategy.pdf.

[USS 99] U.S. SECRETARY OF DEFENSE, "The security situation in the Taiwan straits", 1999. Available at http://www.nti.org/db/china/engdocs/dod0299a.html.

[UWM 11] Uw-Madison, "Information incident reporting and response policy", 2011. Available at http://www.cio.wisc.edu/ireportpolicy.pdf.

[VIO 13] Violino B., "Unseen, all-out cyber war on the U.S. has begun", *Info World*, 2013. Available at http://www.infoworld.com/d/security/unseen-all-out-cyber-war-the-us-has-begun-211438.

[WAL 07] Wall D.S., *Cybercrime: The Transformation of Crime in the Information Age*, Polity, Malden, 2007.

[WAL 08] Wall D.S., "Cybercrime, media and insecurity: the shaping of public perceptions of cybercrime", *International Review of Law, Computers and Technology*, vol. 22, nos.1–2, pp. 45–63, 2008.

[WAL 09] Wall D.S., "The role of the media in generating insecurities and influencing perceptions of cybercrime", in Mesko G., Cockcroft T., Crawford A., Lemaitre A. (eds), *Crime, Media and Fear of Crime*, Tipografija, Ljubljana, pp. 50–76, 2009.

[WIK 11] Wikileaks, "Wikileaks", 2011. Available at http://wikileaks.org/.

[WIL 08] Williams K.S., "Using Tittle's control balance theory to understand computer crime and deviance", *International Review of Law Computers & Technology*, vol. 22, nos. 1–2, pp. 145–155, 2008.

[WIN 08] Winseck D., "Information operations 'Blowback' communication, propaganda and surveillance in the global war on terrorism", *The International Communication Gazette*, vol. 70, no. 6, pp. 419–441, 2008.

[WSB 05] The Economist, "When small is beautifully successful", *The Economist*, 2005. Available at http://www.economist.com/node/5025737.

[WU 06] Wu C., "An overview of the research and development of information warfare in China", Halpin E., Trevorrow P., Webb D., Wright S. (eds), *Cyberwar, Netwar and the Revolution in Military Affairs*, Palgrave Macmillan, New York, pp. 173–195, 2006.

[YAR 06] YAR M., *Cybercrime and Society*, Sage, London, 2006.

[YOU 07] YOUNG J., *The Vertigo of Late Modernity*, Sage, London, 2007.

[ZAV 05] ZAVRSNIK A., "Kibernetična kriminaliteta – (kiber)kriminološke in (kiber)viktimološke posebnosti 'informacijske avtoceste'", *Revija za kriminalistiko in kriminologijo*, vol. 56, no. 3, pp. 248–260, 2005.

[ZAV 07] ZAVRSNIK A., "Vznik kriminologije – 'odkritje' kriminalnega zla v posamezniku", *Revija za kriminalistiko in kriminologijo*, vol. 58, no. 4, pp. 248–260, 2007.

[ZAV 08] ZAVRSNIK A., "Boj za prevlado nad internetom – interno upravljanje in nadzorovanje", *Revija za kriminalistiko in kriminologijo*, vol. 59, no. 4, pp. 321–338, 2008.

[ZAV 10] ZAVRSNIK A., "Criminal justice systems (over)reactions to IT security threats", in BELLINI M. (ed.), *Current Issues in IT Security: Proceedings of the Interdisciplinary Conference*, Duncker & Humblot, Freiburg i. Br./Germany, Berlin, pp. 113–135, 2010.

[ZEP 04] ZEPEP, *Zakon o elektronskem poslovanju in elektronskem podpisu* [ZEPEP-UPB1], Uradni list RS, (98/04), 2004.

Index

Printed and bound by CPI Group (UK) Ltd, Croydon, CR0 4YY